Embraced
by
Compassion

Embraced
by
Compassion

On Human Longing
and Divine Response

Barbara Fiand

CROSSROAD • NEW YORK

1993

The Crossroad Publishing Company
370 Lexington Avenue, New York, NY 10017

Printed in the United States of America

Library of Congress Cataloging-in-Publication Data

Fiand, Barbara.
    Embraced by compassion: on human longing and divine response / Barbara Fiand.
      p. cm.
    Includes bibliographical references.
    ISBN 0-8245-1382-7 (pbk.)
      1. Spiritual life. 2. God. 3. Experience (Religion). I. Title.
BL624.F498   1993
248.4—dc20   93-31855
                                            CIP

Grateful acknowledgment is made to Sigo Press for permission to quote from *Love's Energies* by June Singer and to Bernard J. Boelen for permission to quote from his books *Existential Thinking* and *Personal Maturity*.

To Theresia M. Quigley (Fiand):

Companion from the womb
into the compassion that is God—
with love.

Contents

Preface

Some time ago when I first started to reflect on the theme of this book, a friend of mine shared with me the following dream:

> I found myself in a perfectly square room that had no windows yet was filled with radiance. In the middle of the room stood an ancient, golden urn. I knew it had to be old, for the metal shone in deep rather than glittering brilliance, and the vessel was richly carved. It was quite large and stood on the floor. A solemnity, a sacred presence, permeated the room. Somehow I knew that I stood on holy ground. Approaching the urn, I fell to my knees before it. As I knelt there, a strange sensation befell me. I felt myself being drawn into the vessel and, at the same time, sensed the vessel entering me. We were mysteriously becoming one—the urn and I; I and the urn. I awoke in awe and with a deep feeling of peace. Something sacred had happened, and I would never be the same.

My reaction to my friend's dream was quite similar to hers: I was amazed, awe-struck. I remembered quite suddenly H. A. Guerber's rendition of the appearance of the Holy Grail:

> [G]liding down upon a refulgent beam of celestial light there came a dazzling vision of the Holy Grail. . . . Silent from awe, the knights of the Round Table gazed rapturously at this resplendent vision, 'till at last it vanished as suddenly and as mysteriously as it had come.[1]

Yet my friend's experience had not been quite that way; it had not come from outside her. Her vision, awe-filled though it had been, had not, by vanishing again, required a quest outward, as had the Holy Grail. It had manifested, rather, an inwardness: a presence that was already there, waiting for her to recognize it. It had been *centered,* and had drawn her into union, into the holy that lies deep inside, not above things. It is that holy that urges us to move beyond the distractions of life, calling us home to ourselves from *within,* toward the *more* that will not go away.

But what *really* is this "more"? What is it that breaks into human experience, frequently without warning, and points without compromise into the depth dimension of existence: What is it that haunts us, even in moments of apparent personal "togetherness," with an invitation to go deeper? What is it that invades our life—sometimes through a profound experience of presence, as in the dream, sometimes through agonizing absence? Why are we restless—all of us—searching for more than our here-and-now situation seems to offer? What are we looking for, and why are we looking? This book was written out of the need to explore these questions.

For several years now an introductory graduate course I have been teaching on the relationship of faith to human maturation and freedom has kept my interest centered around what I have come to see as the focal point of the divine-human connection: If Rahner is right and all theology is really anthropology, then the split that for centuries has had us look for God "out there," or "up there," and investigate ourselves "down here"—as beings apart from the Holy, desperately needs to be invalidated. Our search for ourselves somehow *has* to connect us to God, and our search for God will have to be rooted in *our* experience. In fact, I believe God cannot be found anywhere else, and all theological as well as liturgical language that speaks to the contrary ought to be seriously questioned.

These reflections were written over a number of years during which the realization of the human journey as a journey into the God within moved, not always without pain, beyond intellectual platitude into the heart and gut of my life, and "theology by immersion" became the only theology worth living. Life has a way of presenting us with the essentials, of having us meet ourselves unconditionally. This is rarely a tranquil experience, but always, I believe, an experience of God. The following pages are an invitation to engage in this experience. I wish I could say it is easy reading, for I am well aware of the temptation, even among those of us sincerely committed to the religious quest, to go for the simple and to turn away from the difficult; but the fact remains that the real is never easy. Nor is it possible credibly to immerse oneself in the real while remaining within the confines of one discipline alone. Connecting theology meaningfully with anthropology, psychology, and philosophy, however, has its unavoidable moments of struggle. Life often asks us to "marinate" in what we hear and see and feel; to endure it, in other words, with all its confusion. We also have to "marinate" in what we read; to "sit in it," as I suggest to my students; to immerse ourselves in the depth, the pain, and sometimes even the dryness of it, so that the baptism can happen and new life can flow.

The first chapter of this book, "In Search of a Dancing God," is precisely that. It reflects on the dualism of our tradition that, for centuries, has kept God in the realm of the sacred, and has denied the very Incarnation it saw itself proclaiming. Ours has, in many respects, been a theology divided against itself that, in its apparent obsession with speculation and orthodoxy, seems to have deafened itself to the living Word, to have lost its heart. The God of the dance we are searching for is the God of living reality, not of flat definitions—of depth experience rather than mere verbalizations. The God of the dance is the God of the "what if," the God of dreams, the dynamic God of the mystics.

What we are hungering for in the last years of the twentieth century is a retrieval of wonder, a celebration of the mystery that is life itself, and an acceptance of the responsibility and the compassion that accompanies its embrace. Being in step with the dancing God will lead us to this wonder, for it means re-thinking what has been static in order to feel, once again, its life, its rhythm, its relevance, its pain, its glory, as well as our own intrinsic relationships to it all. It means stripping the walls that protect and separate us from the dance, and facing the *who* that we are with relentless honesty. It means being grafted onto the

Christ, experiencing his death, and weaving into our lives the meaning of his resurrection.

Chapter 2, "Embracing the No-Thing," investigates our suitability for such a task. It probes the nature of human openness as the place for faith, and emphasizes our essential emptiness and receptivity to the Holy. It is perhaps the most difficult chapter due to its somewhat philosophical concerns with human existentiality and the specificities of our nature as believers. Its return to the mystical dimension of religion generally may soften the struggle, however, and hopefully illustrate how unified our quest really is.

Chapter 3 on "The Risk of Being Human" concretizes the reflections of Chapter 2 by systematically plotting our growth into wholeness. It shows human development as essentially cyclical—a spiraling process into freedom that surrenders us ever more completely to the breakthrough of God. This chapter will be particularly helpful for obtaining an understanding of faith as a process, rather than as something unchanging that we receive prepackaged. For example, teachers of religion and evangelists will find their intuition confirmed that periods of rejection and an antireligious attitude may be quite normal at certain points in a person's journey into God. These periods do not necessarily imply failure on the part of catechists. There is a flow to the movement of faith that quite readily accommodates such over-againstness. This chapter presents faith development as essentially linked to human maturation with all its periods of crisis and of glory. The religious quest is not an adjunct to our life that we choose or reject; it envelops us virtually from the moment of conception. It is a destiny that sends us forth, whether we are conscious of it or not, and to which we ultimately return after life has challenged us to surrender to the freedom that we are.

"Embraced by Compassion," the fourth and final chapter, addresses most directly the specific concerns that inspired these reflections: a search for the mysterious power that breaks into our lives, haunts us with insatiable longing, and draws us relentlessly beyond ourselves into our innermost being; a search for the initiative underlying, and the response to our yearning; a search for and embrace by God. What seems surprising to many believers and, strangely, to Christian believers as well, is the fact that religious questing is really an essentially dialectic affair, and that the object of our longing in turn longs for us; that God, in fact, creates our longing out of the *longing that God is*; that Love requires love. Chapter 4 explores the meaning of this. It reflects on the wooing of Love, how it manifests itself and entices, and what response it seeks.

Some review of the previous chapters can be found in Chapter 4 in view of the dialectic that it explores. This may help to tidy up and clarify the preceding reflections as well as allow the reader to see their connectedness more explicitly. The questions related to each chapter and found at the end of the book are intended for the same purpose. My hope is that they enhance the meditative process that I see as essential for a successful reading of this book. I am convinced that no reflections on a topic such as this are ever final. Rather, they require an active response—a thoughtful dwelling on the topic and, hopefully, a personal as well as critical appropriation. The questions are presented with this in mind.

I have attempted to write these pages in as inclusive a language style as possible. My reasons for this are not in any way to "make a point" or to appear corrective of a past when social consciousness with respect to women's self-understanding simply was not what it is now. My hope, rather, is to provide women readers of today with as complete an experience of the events discussed in this book as possible. Unfortunately, the matter of inclusion is a somewhat cumbersome task and does not always make for smooth reading, especially in the case of direct citations that have consistently used the third person singular— namely, generic male pronouns. In these situations—except on the rare occasion of a citation from poetry where the insertion of a feminine pronoun would be too disruptive—the generic feminine pronoun has been added or the plural form adopted. My primary objective is at all times to make this book representative of the entire human family. This may mean that at times reading convenience must yield to the value of inclusion, and I beg the reader's support.

Once again there are many who have supported me in my writing and to whom I wish to extend my sincere gratitude. To those participants in my workshops and lectures who have read through the first part of this manuscript and then kept haunting me for the final chapter, thank you for giving me the impetus and energy to keep writing in spite of very serious time constraints. Among the many friends who encouraged me, I am, as always, especially grateful to Clare Gebhardt. Thank you for the sharing, for the dreams, the vision, and for your many, many words of wisdom. To Kay Brogle, thanks for your caring, your interest, and your support; and to Catherine Griffiths, thanks for your faithfulness through it all, and for believing in me. My gratitude, once again, to Crossroad Publishing Company, to Michael Leach, Frank Oveis, Gene Gollogly, and Sr. Mary Margaret, for their continued encouragement and help. And finally, to the students of the Athenaeum of Ohio, especially to members of the famous "Who Am I?" classes; thank you for your enthusiasm, for your boundless energy on behalf of the Gospel, for your challenge and questions, and, most of all, for your generosity and your perseverance.

1

In Search of a Dancing God

I was sitting by the ocean one late summer afternoon, watching the waves rolling in and feeling the rhythm of my breathing, when I suddenly became aware of my whole environment as being engaged in a gigantic cosmic dance. Being a physicist, I knew that the sand, rocks, water, and air around me were made of vibrating molecules and atoms, and that these consisted of particles which interacted with one another. . . . I knew also that the earth's atmosphere was continually bombarded by showers of "cosmic rays," particles of high energy undergoing multiple collisions as they penetrated the air. All this was familiar to me from my research in high-energy physics, but until that moment I had only experienced it through graphs, diagrams, and mathematical theories. As I sat on that beach my former experiences came to life; I "saw" cascades of energy coming down from outer space, in which particles were created and destroyed in rhythmic pulses; I "saw" the atoms of the elements and those of my body participating in this cosmic dance of energy; I felt its rhythm and I "heard" its sound, and at that moment I *knew* that this was the Dance of Shiva, the Lord of Dancers worshiped by the Hindus.[1]

This is how Fritjof Capra begins his book *The Tao of Physics*. His was an experience, he claims, of spiritual insight, of mystical depth, which

15

brought together years of study in the area of quantum physics with the deepest of mystical traditions.

I remember vividly the first time I read this passage. I can still feel the excitement I experienced, the sense of reconciliation and home-coming. Having been reared before Vatican II, I was painfully aware of the chasm that had been established between religion and science from the time of Galileo and before. I had met many a scientist for whom religion belonged to the realm of the esoteric and was of no more significance than magic or fantasy. I had also encountered believ-ers for whom literalism in scripture and doctrine was sacrosanct. It superseded any and all scientific discoveries. One simply swallowed hard and said: "I believe." Interpretation was beyond one's ken. What I was reading here, however, showed me a man who had bridged the gap, a scientist who talked of mysticism and was excited by it. His vision energized me!

My own study of philosophy several years prior to my encounter with Capra had taken me in a similar direction: a movement beyond the purely rational and analytical, into meditative thought,[2] and I felt an immediate kinship with him. I appreciated his acknowledgment of the initial difficulty he had felt in overcoming the divide between the rational and the mystical. I understood the tears that had come with the first approaches of the spiritual in his life, emerging, as it is wont to do, in its own time, "without any effort, . . . from the depth of conscious-ness."[3] I sympathized with his frustration as a writer. He found no dif-ficulty in leading the reader into ever deeper realms of physics, but had to surrender the mystical as an "experience that cannot be learned from books," and admit that "[a] deeper understanding of any mystical tradi-tion can only be felt when one decides to become actively involved in it."[4]

I was first attracted to *The Tao of Physics* by a quote on the back of the Bantam paperback edition that read:

Mystics understand the roots of the *Tao* but not its branches; scientists understand its branches but not its roots. Science does not need mysticism and mysticism does not need science; *but [the human person] needs both.*

It had become clear to me that for centuries Western culture had worked out of the strengths of our diverse expertise—to the detriment of human wholeness. The tragic result of this had been blindness toward each other and an ever deepening split between spirit and matter.

THEOLOGY DIVIDED AGAINST ITSELF

Theology had been of little help in this dilemma. Mystics, as Capra rightly maintains, always played a marginal role in the mainstream of Western thought.[5] Many of them, notably the women, remained largely unnoticed, while their leading male spokespersons frequently suffered church condemnation and silencing. Christian theology, especially after Augustine, adopted almost exclusively the language and "mind" of Greek metaphysics with its rational and speculative approach. In due time it identified itself as a science, claiming its own independent explicative scheme in which the mysteries of the faith could be systematically surveyed, indifferent to time and historical context.[6] In this way theology may have hoped to gain respectability in an increasingly science-oriented West, but, at the same time, it progressively lost its connection with the mystery it purported to serve. Today, according to James J. Bacik, we are facing an eclipse of mystery. "A significant number of people in the Western World . . . are impoverished by a diminished or distorted sense of the mysterious depths of human existence."[7] Bacik suggests that the theologians' primary mandate consists in attending "to the often neglected task of disclosing and articulating the mystery dimension implicit in all human experience so that Christian doctrines can be related to genuine human concerns."[8]

Perhaps a more radical proposal—sadly, a more realistic one—would be to challenge theologians to the task of discovering the mystery first for themselves. In today's "eclipse," it is not at all a foregone conclusion that the one engaged in the theological enterprise encounters, is engaged with, and embraces the object of his or her investigation. Whereas "the verb 'I believe'/*credo* in the early Church did not signify a theoretical activity of the mind, nor . . . in any sense refer to the acceptance of a series of propositions,"[9] the deductive frame of mind to which the science of theology has given itself for centuries now leaves it questionable whether today the "heart" task of actual faith surrendered to the mystery can simply be assumed when theology is operative.

> The verb "I believe"/*credo* is a compound of the noun *cor* (*cordis*), meaning heart, and the verb *do*, to put, place, set, which is distinct from though related to the other verb *do* (*dare*), to give. Thus the root meaning of "I believe"/*credo* is "I set my heart on." "I give my heart to." Taken in the context of the New Testament and used in association with baptism and the early creeds, "I believe"/*credo* meant "I hereby commit myself," "I pledge myself." . . . When used in reference to the early creeds, "I believe"/*credo*, contrary to popular understanding, was not primarily addressed to propositional statements. Instead "I believe"/*credo* was about the activity of becoming involved and engaged with God.[10]

Theology today, it seems to me, almost exclusively concerns itself with the specific *content of faith*, quite distinct from the *act of faith*. Furthermore, it blurs this separation by subsuming the latter under the former. As Dermot A. Lane points out, a gradual separation between these two essential aspects of any viable religion occurred in Christendom somewhere around the seventeenth century.

> Believing *in* God became synonymous with believing *that* God. . . . This development, or more accurately distortion, hardened in the nineteenth century with the result that in the twentieth century the act of faith, in many instances, had become identified with the content of faith.[11]

The articulation, explication, and even the assent to theoretical expression is, however, primarily an intellectual exercise. It can happen with very little, if any, commitment, allowing for our personal *yes* to the living God to be easily and painlessly replaced by conceptual frameworks and contextualizations. Thus the energy and power of the divine-human relationship flickers low and the mystery is eclipsed. "So-called 'scientific' theology," Dorothee Soelle tells us in her book *The Strength of the Weak*,

> usually expresses itself in language void of consciousness. . . . [I]t is empty of emotion, insensitive to human experience, ghostlike, neutral, uninteresting, unappealing, flat. It admits of no doubt, which is to say it represses the shadow side of faith and does not lift it into consciousness.[12]

It lacks the passion and reality of life, hence, of the living God. As such, it fails to inspire. "You cannot reach people if you are divorced from your own emotions."[13]

AUTHENTIC FAITH

Lane insists that authentic faith, in contrast, is "insight into the truth of God followed by a *personal response* to that insight which *affects daily living*."[14] It is not the passive acquiescence to, nor the dry proclamation of, truths without any personal involvement. Neither is it mere personal opinion about what appears to be "intellectually shaky and dubious" (a further distortion contributed to this discussion by twentieth-century relativism).

> Faith is a personal participation at all levels of life in the truth of God. Faith is a recognition of God that *alters our life-styles*. Faith, therefore, is primarily a *practical affair*, especially in its effects, rather than a purely theoretical stance.
> Faith is a decision to enter into a personal relationship with God. This relationship is one of love, trust, and confi-

dence addressed to God as personal. . . . Faith is an act of sur-render to God, a *placing of one's heart and one's affections in God.* Faith is, therefore, an act of the whole person involving intellect and will as well as emotions and feelings.

Faith is an act that changes the individual; it brings about conversion, a conversion that touches the whole outlook and attitude of the individual. . . . [Faith] is the experience of living before, in, and around the presence of God.

The act of faith is always addressed to God, not as a scientific formula but as a *living personal reality* that is active in the world and in our lives.[15]

Faith is the condition for authentic theology that, in turn, articulates it, but it can never be reduced to theology or its belief-statements. Whereas faith is committed to the mystery in its "unconcealing concealment" (Heidegger)—its eternal revealing and withholding—theology addresses the revelation of that mystery in time and in culture. It can be said that theology is a means to faith, but, paradoxically, it can be so only if first it is held in faith and finds its roots there, as the living, vibrating ground for the unfathomable mystery of the Holy.

THE NEED FOR MYSTICS

To be viable mystagogues, therefore, as Bacik would have them, that is, to be those who initiate others into a perception and appreciation of the mystery dimension of their experience,[16] theologians need first to re-ground themselves in the mystery and must learn to dwell there, no matter how uncomfortable this may be initially. Theologians, quite simply, must become mystics. Karl Rahner expresses the urgency of this matter when, in *The Practice of Faith*, he points out that "the Christian of the future will be a mystic or he or she *will not exist at all.*"[17] Rahner holds mysticism to be possible for every authentic believer. It is "a genuine experience of God emerging from the very heart of our existence."[18]

The classical definition of mysticism confirms this interpretation. It identifies mysticism as a "perception of God through experience," implying, as Soelle explains, that, for the mystic, the awareness of God is gained not primarily through books or the authority of religious teachings, "but through the life experiences of human beings, experiences that are articulated and reflected upon in religious language but that *first come to people in what they encounter in life.*"[19]

A distinction that Dorothee Soelle makes between a deductive and an inductive approach to theology may be of help here. It is her contention that depth theology begins in pain. With Kierkegaard she holds that "sickness unto death," or, as she puts it, "our need for more, . . . our sense of failure, . . . our awareness of life destroyed, . . . [of the reign of God] that is not yet here,"[20] of the need for a "clean heart," is the only viable starting point for any meaningful theological activity today.

It is senseless merely to theologize deductively with credal statements such as: "I believe in God, the Father almighty." "In the beginning God created the heavens." ". . . sits at the right hand of God the Father almighty." "I believe in one, holy, catholic Church." Theoretically interesting though these statements may be, by themselves they do not speak to the heart. They evoke yawns rather than zeal. Quite a different result would occur, however, if we permitted another sort of statement into the theological arena, a statement of human experience, of our existential reality, of induction: "Mrs. Smith has been waiting for seventeen months for an 8-by-12-foot room in a nursing home." "The cosmetic industry was able to increase its sales in this area by 40 percent."[21] "We will all need to go on a diet after our Christmas feasting." "We need to cut out lunch programs in inner city schools to reduce the national deficit."

If, as John Francis Kavanaugh insists, "a 'gospel' is a book of revelation, an ultimate source of reference wherein we find ourselves revealed, . . . a response to the questions of who we are, what we may hope for, how we may aspire to act, what endures, what is important, what is of true value,"[22] then a theology, effectively concerned with our Gospel, needs to address us *there*. "Do you believe in God?" is not as important a question as "What god do you believe in?"[23] This is not a simplistic suggestion to replace theology with the social sciences (although I must insist that it should certainly not lose touch with them, remaining compartmentalized and esoteric, and developing what John Macquarrie calls a "Sunday mentality" over against an "every day mentality"[24]). Rather, it is a serious plea to ground theology, without compromise, in the human condition where, alone, our relationship with the divine can become real.

It is my conviction that when theology faces the lived reality of human existence in all its brokenness, its language changes. "Create in me a clean heart, O God," "Have mercy on me, O God, in your goodness," "Out of the depths I cry to you," then become statements of theological significance, not just for writings or courses on the psalms, but also and primarily because of theology's fundamental and passionate concern for, as well as involvement with the divine-human interaction that is our life in faith. Unfortunately, the calcification of speculative theology has become so prevalent in modern times, and a consequent divorce of professed faith and the practice of personal as well as social justice seems so widely evident, that an effective "return to the heart," or conversion, appears to be possible only through an encounter, or perhaps more strongly put, through a direct confrontation with human brokenness—what Soelle calls "negative forces."[25] I am referring here to a necessary and overwhelming recognition of one's own connectedness with—and responsibility for—social evil and its direct opposition to the goodness of God's creative plan. One has to experience, if you will, the crisis of personal involvement with the inconsistencies in professed Gospel living. One has to see that "All is not right with one's world," and to know that one's own hands are also unclean.

Theology begins with experience and sets experience over against the promise of a whole life, the promise of the [reign] of God. It confronts [negative forces] with the genuine life that has been promised us, which is no more nor less than everything for all of us. And only if we engage in this kind of theology can we rediscover the language Jesus used. His language was not deductive either; he did not begin with established principles.[26]

Jesus had no patience with banality and mediocrity. In his death and resurrection he modeled for us *our* story, not as a clean and neat theological thesis, but as having to be worked out in the blood, sweat, and tears, as well as in the moments of ecstasy that comprise the human condition.

The theologian as mystic in contemporary society, rather than being lost in rapture, will be held in the travail of the Spirit of Jesus groaning within him or her for the transformation of the world in Christ. By no means will this be easy. Quite clearly, it requires a solitary journey; a personal decision of surrender in the face of one's own finitude; an abandon, linked at the same time with resolve in the knowledge that God's "strength is made perfect in [our] weakness" (2 Cor 12:9).

THEOLOGY BY IMMERSION

The critical honesty to which the inductive approach calls us in contemporary times, is never without compassion both for ourselves and for the world. Nor is it ever without passion. Besides radically addressing itself to every facet of our own lives and challenging us to ever greater integrity, inductive theology also fundamentally transforms our creeds, our doctrines and dogmas. It immerses them, as it were, in experience—an experience, it must be noted, that is valid not necessarily because of its exclusive encounter with goodness and justice, but because of its longing for them. Thus, for example, whereas the credal profession of faith in "one, holy, catholic, and apostolic Church" might deductively remain quite dry and even ring blindly triumphalistic, its immersion into our lived reality of shameful exclusivism, persecution of diversity, hierarchism, and dualism, as well as into our urgent longing for reconciliation and healing, renders this belief-statement markedly dynamic. It brings to consciousness the breakthrough of God in diversity and, therefore, encompasses a wide spectrum of believing humanity. It calls us toward the authentically and fundamentally egalitarian society of our earliest heritage in Jesus' "discipleship of equals."[27] It urges movement away from dualistic, patriarchal distinctions, and toward the wholeness that truly is holiness. This statement, encountered inductively, speaks of eschatological urgency, of the reign of God that is here but not yet, of God's dwelling place for which we are responsible.

On the level of doctrine, induction can also do much to revitalize meaning. Thus, reflection on the Trinity, for example, can virtually transform glazed stares of incomprehension and bring about not only fascination but also commitment on the part of students when it is entered into inductively. Karl Rahner is right in his observation that

> although most Christians believe the doctrine because it has been taught them, *it makes no real difference to their life of faith.* . . . [W]hen most Christians are called back to the doctrine of the Trinity and asked to say what it means, they present themselves as . . . "tritheists," i.e., believers in three Gods,[28]

although they claim to believe only in one God. It is clear that their response is to a doctrine taught but not contextualized into contemporary experience, hence, to a credal statement of no significance to them. Rahner holds that their confusion arises because of the term "person," which has come to be experienced as an "independent center of consciousness and freedom," in today's world. "Three persons," therefore, means "three individuals." This was not the meaning of the Greek words *hypostasis* and *prosopon,* which today might much more accurately be translated as "way of being,"[29] rather than "person."

With this clarification, the doctrine could perhaps assume for us, once again, the importance that ought to be given it in the Christian tradition. D. M. Baillie puts it well: To the question: What is distinctive about the Christian God? He answers: The belief that God is trinitarian, and that God is love. He then points out that both observations are really one and the same: "The Christian doctrine of the Trinity means that God is love, i.e., that God chooses not to remain self-enclosed, but to reach out graciously to humankind in Son and Spirit."[30] The breakthrough of God into creation is brought home to us, made visible, and articulated by God's personal entry into history in Christ Jesus. It remains a reality that sustains us and gives us life through the Spirit of Jesus calling us ever to be co-creators, to be echoes of God's love, because of the Christ event in which we are held.

Baillie's explanation invites us to move beyond abstract, philosophical speculation about a far-removed deity. We are touched in our experience: "The graciousness of the mystery we call God (Father) reaching out to us" and touching us from the very depths of God's very being:

> [T]he doctrine of the Trinity in meaningful English today could be stated in these terms: The one God has three ways of being. . . .
> Trinitarian thinking arose from the *religious experience* of the followers of Jesus. They experienced God in an incarnate or historically concrete way in Jesus, and they experienced God in a spiritual way in the depth of their own spirit.[31]

They called the mysterious energy that Jesus witnessed to them as love Father. The incarnation of this love in time and space they called Son, and the abiding presence of this love they called Spirit. The strength of their experience is attested to in Scripture:

> We encounter God in the depths of ourselves, empowering us spiritually, grounding our faith, hope, and love, endowing us with gifts to help others (1 Cor 12 and 13), making Father and Son present (Jn 15:23), reminding us of the things Jesus said and clarifying them for us (Jn 16:12–14), uniting us with other believers into one social body (1 Cor 12:12–13), praying in us with unspeakable groanings (Rm 8:26–27). This is an experience of God's own self too, occurring in our person-

al depths. We call it "God the Holy Spirit." God is one, and what we have described is our complex experience of God. It is the basis of our knowledge of God as trinitarian.[32]

It is the core of our faith, the root reason for the greatest commandment, the heart of all creative energy in establishing God's reign. It is endangered when excessive dogmatism imprisons it in verbiage, thus isolating it and impoverishing all of Christian self-understanding.

The scope of this reflection does not allow for an in-depth discussion on the power of the trinitarian doctrine, nor is this the intent. What I merely wish to illustrate here is the energy flowing within a theology that comes from immersion. Our concern revolves around the need for direct and honest experience in any viable theological endeavor. We will recall Rahner's exhortation that mysticism is essential for the survival of Christianity. For this reason he advocates the disclosing of the mystery as a primary theological task.

SPIRALLING INWARD

Rahner addresses Dorothee Soelle's distinction between inductive and deductive theology no less radically, but perhaps more directly or more clearly at its source. Whereas the concern for justice and the transformation of all things in Christ is undoubtedly at the heart of Christianity and is, therefore, clearly of primary inspirational importance, as Soelle rightly illustrates, it would seem to me unlikely that it stands at the beginning of the individual Christian's conscious journey. No one is born with a clear sense of justice. We grow into it. The travail that is life prunes us for it in our drive toward wholeness. "The activity of becoming involved and engaged with God," which constitutes authentic believing,[33] is, therefore, not an activity that can be exercised with full and equal freedom right from the beginning.

In his book *Personal Maturity*, Bernard J. Boelen sees the human being as fundamentally "freedom in the process of freeing itself."[34] Although baptized into the Christ Event very early in life, we begin to understand ourselves as Christians only progressively. Rather than being on a straight, narrow, and predictable road, we are an ever spiraling movement into God, very much like Maria Harris describes it:

> [A] rhythmic series of movements, which, unlike the steps of a *ladder* or a *staircase*, do not go up and down. Instead the steps of *our* lives are much better imagined as steps in a dance, where there is movement backward and forward, turn and return, bending and bowing, circling and spiraling, and no need to finish and move on to the next step, except in our own good time, and God's. At whatever step we find ourselves, we are where we are meant to be. Leaning into and living into any one of the steps is the only way to understand it, and moving on to a next one happens according to our soul's own rhythm—in ways similar to the bodily rhythms natural to . . . women.[35]

We encounter God at diverse levels of depth, timely in their own way. These levels are interspersed with numerous plateaus, periods of fixation, betrayals, and also repentance, and deeper releasement. The pain that Soelle identifies as the starting point of all authentic theology can, therefore, be understood in a very real sense as the pain of our own freeing process. It is a necessary pain, as is the pain in a woman's body as it gives itself to the cycle of life. It is the pain of breaking open through the crusts of human conditioning, socialization, and stratification—through numerous cultural barriers of resistance and personal masks.

Undoubtedly, as was stressed already, our co-being and, therefore, our social responsibility will always be part of our inner journey, since we are inextricably linked to others. Authentic brotherhood and sisterhood with humankind is, however, grounded in a primary depth experience that, even though never totally isolated, has to be endured in the solitary resolve of each person's own unique and unrepeatable quest for the ultimate.

It is here, I believe, where Rahner begins, and, although for some the radical encounter with what Jung calls the "Self" may appear as unnecessary "navel gazing," it is, nevertheless, a fact that a fundamental and honest encounter with one's own core is prerequisite for justice. Without it, the "bandwagon" approach to social concerns can quite easily take hold of even the most pious endeavor. Sebastian Moore is right. The "who am I?" question *is* "the question to God."[36]

In my own classes I usually begin the difficult process of explaining what Rahner calls "transcendental" experience with a probing of this question. The functional responses that our culture so glibly substitutes for depth are not easily abandoned here, and it seems much simpler to identify oneself with the criteria of name, occupation, age, domicile, nationality, degree, and gender than to allow oneself to encounter the enigma of one's inner core. There is a bit of the "Hound of Heaven" experience in all of this, and the maieutic of letting the self appear in its vast emptiness and stillness can be quite disconcerting. Nevertheless, this is where Rahner points for the primitive experience of God, and hence, for the starting point of theology. In an essay dealing specifically with the experience of God, Rahner urges the reader to face first and foremost his or her inner movements, his or her depth reality; to encounter pain there, and to embrace it silently without straining for explanations and rationalizations:

> Be still for once. Don't try to think of so many complex and varied things. Give these deeper realities of the spirit a chance now to rise to the surface: silence, fear, the ineffable longing for truth, for love, for fellowship, for God. Face loneliness, fear, imminent death! *Allow such ultimate, basic human experiences to come first.* Don't go talking about them, making up theories about them, but simply *endure these basic experiences*. Then in fact something like a primitive awareness of God can emerge. Then perhaps we cannot say much about it; then what we "grasp" first of all about God appears to be nothing, to be the absent, the nameless, absorbing and suppressing all that can be expressed and conceived.

If we do not learn slowly in this way to enter more and more into the company of God and to be open to [God], if we do not constantly attempt to reflect in life *primitive experiences of this kind—not deliberately intended or deliberately undertaken*—and from that point onward to realize them more explicitly in the religious act of meditation and prayer, of solitude and the *endurance of ourselves, if we do not develop such experiences*, then our religious life is and remains really of secondary character and its conceptual-thematic expression is false; then we talk of God as if we had already slapped [God] on the shoulder—so to speak—and, in regard to [humans], we feel that we are God's supervisors and more or less [God's] equals: the result is that, for all our preaching, we ultimately lack credibility for the [people] of today and for those who really count. Whenever piety is directed by an ingenious, complicated intellectuality and conceptuality, with highly complicated theological tenets, it is really a pseudo-piety, however profound it seems to be.[37]

POINTING INTO THE MYSTERY

Only when there is nothing left for us to speculate about, and the encounter with the depth of our humanity has rendered us utterly speechless, is there appropriate room for the all-encompassing embrace of the Holy One. Only then, be it in ecstasy or in agony, are we opened to the radical experience of ourselves as pointers into the mystery, no more and no less.

It may, of course, not be immediately clear how the "who am I?" question provides us with such depth. As Rahner rightly points out: "[T]his primitive, nameless and themeless experience is apparently wholly repressed and buried by our daily routine, by all that we otherwise have to do." There is, furthermore, no guarantee that, once surfaced and probed, it cannot at some point "be buried again even through our theological, ascetic and pious chatter."[38]

In the chapters that follow, we will attempt to unpack in greater detail the different levels of, and opportunities for, growth through which our search for our deepest center passes. For the time being it will be necessary to accept without deeper discussion that humans, quite simply, are transcendent by nature. "Persons as spiritual subjects possess an essential reference to absolute mystery which is always present whether they explicitly recognize it or not and whether they accept it or reject it."[39] Thomas Merton puts it boldly when he identifies us as "a gap, an emptiness that calls for fulfillment from someone else, and the very nature of our being as creatures implies this sense of a need to be completed by [the one] from whom we come."[40] It seems that there is within our very being a pointing beyond ourselves: "[O]ur self-experience always includes an intentional surpassing of individual limitations and raises the question about the source of this power."[41] It is of interest, furthermore, to observe that the question into the *who* that I am, once it has let go of functional criteria and has faced its own inner emptiness, invariably goes deeper into the *why* of it all and, as I discover that I do not have within myself the reason for my own existence nor am I able to find it specifically in any other human being—including my own parents, ancestors, country, or race, an even greater emptiness opens up for me.

Sartre identifies this experience as a "useless suffering," to which humans are condemned by the integrity of their being transcendent.[42] It is, of course, entirely possible to conclude that, if humans do not have the reason for their own existence within themselves, there *is* no reason. Atheistic humanism and the "Theater of the Absurd" in twentieth-century drama attest to this conclusion as widespread today. This, however, does not have to be the whole story. It is equally possible to refuse to come to closure this quickly and simplistically; to move, instead, into this extraordinary void of our experience and there to allow ourselves to embrace still deeper questions; to be fascinated by, rather than discouraged with, our own transcendence in spite of its inherent suffering, and consciously to allow the latter to be complemented by "a dynamic striving in which our knowing and willing are never brought to rest by any particular achievement but constantly press toward the infinite."[43]

The pain experienced in our own limitations, and in the inability to find the "enough" either in things or in personal relationships "is concretized and sharpened by the tragic experiences of life such as failed love, suffering, sickness, and the final limit: death. In these boundary situations," as Karl Jaspers calls them, "we experience ourselves as limited, finite, and contingent. However, we can only experience these events as limited because in some way we have already transcended them."[44] Hence, in spite of their negativity, they carry promise. Just as a slave knows his or her oppression only because he or she is essentially called to freedom and *is*, even if not in the present situation, nevertheless fundamentally and inherently free, so humans know their finitude because the infinite is already beckoning them beyond their limitations. They hold within themselves the transcendent as the source of their frustrations with their essential finitude as well as of ever empowering hope.

GRAFTED INTO THE CHRIST

I have already pointed out that the pain experienced here can be identified as another way of seeing what Soelle called the starting point for all authentic theology. One could be discouraged at this point by the seeming emphasis on negativity, but this is not an unhealthy craving for suffering, nor a revisiting of the punishing God of more primitive, masochistic tendencies in theology. We will remember that Capra's story, cited at the beginning of this chapter and telling of his encounter with a dancing universe and, through it, with Shiva, the "Lord of Dancers," mentions both creation and destruction. Shiva is also the destroyer god, a god well acquainted with pain, but in a creative, not a sadistic way.

Only a dualistic outlook can misjudge the reality of pain in the growth process that is life and, instead of accepting its value, condemn it as punishment. Anyone who sees heaven as "eternal bliss hereafter," will interpret our sojourn here on earth, in contra-distinction, as the "valley of darkness and tears." If the former is good and holy, the latter is wrought with evil. We have insisted, however, that pain is part of the passion that is our openness to meaning—our existence. As such, it is of the essence of our humanity. Nor is it merely human. Pain, as "tragic conflict," so the Russian philosopher Nicolas Berdyaev tells us, is even of God. Here Berdyaev is not talking of Shiva but, in fact, of the depth of our very own tradition. The following summarizes his views:

> The God and Creator of life possesses the attributes of life holistically. S/He is dynamic not immobile, flowing out in Self-gift and yearning for all things to return to Him/Her. God is revealed in our Christian tradition as "sacrificial love" which, "far from suggesting self-sufficiency implies the need of passing into its 'other.' " Sacrifice implies tragedy and tragedy implies pain. If the Christian God is a God of sacrificial love (a truth no believer can deny), then pain—the birth-pain which opens to fullness of life—is Creator pain.[45]

Now it is precisely this pain that is at issue here. The pain that sets into motion all authentic theological reflection is also the pain that grounds us in the death and the resurrection of the Christ. As members of Christ's church we are grafted into his pain and into his glory. We are held in the pain of the breakthrough of God's love that will permit no shortcuts, and allows only for the full surrender of everything into divine nothingness where alone the fullness of God's love is revealed. "Your attitude must be that of Christ [who] emptied himself" (Phil 2:5–7).

THE RESURRECTION INSIGHT

And what happens to us when, in the passion of our quest, we allow the stripping of our own functional identity to open us up to vulnerability? What happens when we surrender to the pain and to the death, to the destruction? The answer comes to us out of the depth of the empty tomb: "The reason for your existence is my passionate love. You are because I love You!" "God chose us in [Christ] before the world began" (Eph 1:4). "Love, then, consists in this: not that we have loved God, but that [God] has loved us" (1 Jn 4:10). Now "Go into the whole world and proclaim the good news to all creation" (Mk 16:15).

It has surprised me in my teaching and lecturing experiences how rarely this resurrection insight, with which the Scriptures are filled, finds its way into my listeners' responses when we probe the "why am I" question together and attempt to move to its ultimate limits. It is as if the primary and unconditional love of God amazes and surprises twentieth-century Christians almost as much as it did the outcasts, tax collectors, prostitutes, and sinners of Jesus' day. The message proclaimed by Jesus witnessed to an inner freedom and authority that astounded his followers. His charisma intoxicated, as well as convinced them. His "God-intimacy,"[46] as Sebastian Moore calls it, was entirely revolutionary; his human intimacy wooed them and won them; his concern for God's reign put their hearts on fire. That is why his death shattered them so, and that is why his resurrection is the cornerstone of our faith. In it "the 'abandoned' prophet was raised and his message vindicated, namely, *that the Lover-God will not be denied* and that the freedom that this opens up for God's people is real. *God has loved us with an everlasting love.*"[47]

The fact that the truth of this insight so rarely seems to speak to the experience of Christians today is a sad commentary on what Moore identifies as the "gap between the 'normal' and the true."[48] Sin, he insists, is "the unreality of God."[49] It belongs to the banal, the controllable, the normal, all too normal. It lacks the risk-taking called for by truth; the joy and excitement of encountering the new, and the trust and the peace that follows it, as one moves into closer union with the goal of all one's striving; the buoyancy of "surpassing" mere finitude in reaching beyond and touching the Holy; the experience of one's transcendence in all its positive aspects; the bliss of being held by God. Sin is lost in death. It is boring. Sin does not touch the heart at its core and, therefore, cannot energize it. Sin is alienation, being torn from one's center, being lost and needing to be found.

It is my sense that contemporary Christianity is, in many ways, floundering in this banality and has lost the enthusiasm (Latin: *en-theos*, "being in God") of the resurrection. Perhaps in the hedonist and consumerist mind-set (or "heart-set") of today, we have allowed ourselves to resist pain for so long that we can no longer bring ourselves to accept with ease and truly to live in the ecstasy of our faith. Rahner is right: We *need* to be mystics, lest we perish. We need to enter into the truth of the resurrected Christ, allow ourselves to be embraced there by the compassion of God and, thus, to be changed.

LOVE CASTS OUT FEAR

Not long ago, during Sunday morning worship, I saw a young black man holding his infant daughter in his arms. The little one seemed fascinated with her father's voice. She had placed her face square in front of his and was watching his lips. The young man was swinging rhythmically with the music, almost dancing with his child. Gurgling with delight, she placed her little fingers on his lips and finally put almost her entire hand into his mouth, totally secure in his love. The image of this child's joy and safety in her father's presence was a powerful prayer experience for me.

I wonder if what prevents so many of us from letting ourselves be free, or at least, what seems to make it so difficult for us to accept the resurrection process, is not a deep-down insecurity, a fear and mistrust of God's blessings. Our contemporary Christian dislike and misunderstanding of pain seems matched only by our suspicion of happiness even, paradoxically, as we crave it.

A story was told in antiquity that may apply today with unusual accuracy: It is said of Polycrates, ruler of Samos, that he was the luckiest man of his time. For him every endeavor resulted in success. So favored was he, in fact, that his friends became alarmed for him, not because they were jealous, but because they feared the gods would be. They feared divine resentment of his prosperity, respect, and power and worried that the gods would punish him with suffering. They advised him that, in order to avert the anger of the gods, he should divest himself of some of his fortune. We are told that Polycrates, following their advice, threw his most precious ring into the ocean to appease the gods, only to have fishermen unwittingly retrieve it for him from the belly of a fish. Polycrates became so alarmed at his unmitigated blessings, and so fearful of divine displeasure, that ultimately his fortune became his curse.

We find in this story the ancients' symbol for the indissoluble tie that existed for them between good fortune and fear of punishment—a tie that, strangely enough, has persisted through the ages and has permeated our Western self-understanding even to this day. Is it not true that for many of us, regardless of contemporary attempts at a more positive approach, there seems to be a basic mistrust of personal well-being? Whereas renunciation, self-abnegation, dedication, and hard work are held in high esteem (partly, I suspect, because the sufferings that accompany them are largely self-chosen, hence controllable), when things go well for us we grow wary. "The God who loves us," we say, "chastises us," and, although success is often seen as a sign of God's favor and our righteousness in God's eyes, yet, paradoxically, too much success becomes suspect: "Things are going too well. Something is bound to happen."

What is it that has brought about this attitude? Few of us have ever heard of Polycrates, yet what Dorothee Soelle calls "polycratic fear,"[50] pervades our reality, and prevents both our celebration and the sharing of our blessings. Even if, for the most part, no longer theologically proclaimed as such, the God of a large part of Western Christendom seems, nevertheless, to be a jealous God and, as such, speaks much more forcefully to our behavior patterns than does the God in whose eyes we are precious; who loves us, and rejoices in human fulfillment and well-being; the God unto whose lips we can put our fingers and with whom we can dance and sway to the music of our lives.

There may, of course, be many reasons for polycratic fear today. The social analysis that Dorothee Soelle offers is significant. She suggests that "[i]n a society in which all essential relationships are determined by the laws of conflict and competition, even the fortuitous

well-being of an individual always appears to be possible only parasiti-
cally."[51] We are consumers at heart.

> And since we are accustomed to ask of everything that con-
> fronts us, What does it cost? and, Who pays for it? this ques-
> tion cannot be kept out of even the most private realms; it is
> the contemporary formulation of polycratic fear. We experi-
> ence fulfillment as something that is stolen; the more success-
> ful we are, the more like thieves we feel.[52]

As such we stand condemned by our own mercantilism which pervades even our spirituality, fills us with guilt, and makes us incapable
of gratitude. We measure all things according to the dictates of a
workaday world, a world of production and the protection of assets.
Soelle's analysis ought not to be underestimated. Religion, no matter
how divinely inspired, takes its expression, nevertheless, within a
social context. If I must shield myself from my neighbor, ultimately I
will feel I must have to hide from my God also. A neighbor whose
envy I must fear, invariably points beyond himself or herself to a jealous God before whom, also, I stand condemned.

It is clear that Soelle's analysis is pertinent to our times and must,
therefore, be taken seriously. I do believe, however, that there is a still
deeper issue here, and that what one might identify as an economic
analysis does not address the divine-human dynamic foundationally
enough. It would seem to me that, contrary to what Marx proposes,
economic structures ultimately grow out of human self-understanding
(of which the religious impetus is an integral part), not vice versa.
Though the potential for human development and wholeness is certainly enhanced by favorable economic structures, and the absence of conflict and competition there would clearly do much for human maturation, these structures, albeit important, are only means and never the
reason for cultural and individual growth, health, and wholeness. Thus,
although socio-economic paradigms have certainly changed numerous
times since Polycrates was king of Samos, we stand shoulder to shoulder with him today in our basic mistrust of good fortune and in our fear

of eventual deprivation and punishment visited upon us from forces beyond our control and attributed frequently to God.

Even though Jesus has come to proclaim God's favor to all peoples, and God's reign not only in the hereafter but very clearly in the here and now, many of us hear this message only theoretically, while in our hearts we continue to project the spirit of over-againstness and competitiveness onto each other and even onto God. The reason for this, as I see it, is a lack of conversion that needs to be addressed from a base that is broader than mere economics or even sociology. It is a concern for anthropology, since it pertains, as I see it, to the evolution of the human psyche as a whole.

Consumerism and competitiveness are only aspects of a general and all-pervading disposition or attitude—a spirit of the age—a mode of consciousness—that glorifies functionality and sees measurability, calculation, objectification, and control as the primary and even the sole criteria for reality. This mode of consciousness has pervaded Western thought for a period estimated to be between three to five thousand years now,[53] and places the antiquity of Polycrates, therefore, well within our time. Modes of human functionality, domination, calculation, and exchange have certainly varied during these years; what has not changed is the *fundamental disposition out of which human perception and consequent behavior patterns arise.* Human action flows from vision. Modes of consciousness identify our humanity and its evolution. Though theoretically sound, a divine-human dynamic that points on the emotional and experiential level to fear and ultimate mistrust needs to be examined at its foundations.

In the following chapters (especially Chapter 3), we will look more closely at this fundamental disposition, attempt to understand it, and assess its influence on religious self-understanding. We all know that the beginning of healing lies in the recognition of brokenness. If we are to be resurrection people—not only deductively but inductively as well, down to the very marrow of our bones—the "gap between the 'normal' and the true" needs further challenge. It is time for a revolution of consciousness: "a gestalt shift in the whole way of seeing our relations to one another [and to God] so that our behavior patterns are reformed from the inside out."[54] This means, first and foremost, that we face the resistance in our own inner depths, understand it within the wider sphere of basic human development, and parallel this with cultural evolution. Authentic change in perception happens only once we can embrace our past creatively toward the future. The God with whom we will feel secure enough to enter into both the pleasure and the pain of life, on whom we can set our heart, to whom we can commit ourselves, whose presence is real, who speaks to us in our time, the God of the mystics, the God of Jesus Christ awaits us there.

2

Embracing the No-Thing

Your attitude must be that of Christ [who] emptied himself and took the form of a slave being born in the likeness of [humankind]. (Phil 2:5,7)

Whenever one begins to reflect on the possibility of faith—the what of it, its why, and its where—it is wise to meditate on this passage from Paul's letter to the Philippians. There is a direct correlation, I believe, between being authentically human and being persons of faith, and the crux of the correlation can be found precisely in the Christ activity recommended here: "He emptied himself." From this self-emptying, Paul suggests, flowed the authenticity of all subsequent attitudes and behavior, and ultimately, therefore, "God exalted him."

THE PLACE FOR FAITH

What is it that makes faith possible for us? Although we attribute faithfulness to dogs or horses, it is clear that animals do not experience faith as such. When the psalmist exhorts sun and moon, as well as all living things, to bless Yahweh, we know that he or she is really the agent here. Praise breaks out in *us*. We do not expect our heart's exultation to be appreciated by inanimate things, nor by living creatures that lack inwardness. We look at creation, we see the self-revelation of

God there, and we burst forth in benediction. Creation is gathered together, if you will, in *our* prayer and worship.

No one denies, of course, that the beauty of the world outside, of animals and nature, is a catalyst for wonder and praise, but the *place* for worship is in the human heart. Faith happens in us. Why? Contrary to what might be expected, in an age of quick solutions and easy definitions, this question is not easily addressed, because, as with all things holy, it moves us into the divine-human dynamic that is never clearcut. It touches issues of relationship, of freedom as well as surrender—issues that defy neat categories and conditions. Its answer must be pondered carefully, and reveals itself slowly in an unfolding process that requires meditation on, and exploration into both the human and the divine at work (or play) there.

To ready ourselves for this process in the simplest manner I can think of, and to clear away right from the start some unnecessary difficulties, it may be of help to let go of seeing faith as *a* gift and as something we subsequently *have* or possess—as the property or possession of God, passed on to us in the form of a particular virtue. We might want to move instead toward understanding it as an occurrence, an *event that gifts us*, that overwhelms us, in fact, and holds us; as something in which we dwell, yes, even more intimate perhaps, as something we *are*, and as something made possible in our very being because of our nature as *persons*.

THE MEANING OF PERSON

It is interesting to note that the word "person" is derived from the Latin *personare* (*per*, through; *sonare*, to sound). The etymology of this word reveals much about the wisdom of the ancients in whom language first broke forth and found expression—about their insight into the authenticity and beauty of their own being as receptive, vulnerable, and interdependent. Imaging with our foremothers and forefathers into the nature of personhood as that "through which sound flows," invariably returns me to Caryll Houselander's *The Reed of God*: I think of the emptiness of the Mother of God, praised here in the fullness of her humanity as person, and symbolized by a wind instrument, a flute. There are certain distinct characteristics that allow for sound to flow through a flute. First, it would seem that a flute must be *open* to receive the breath of the flutist. It will also have to be hollow or *empty within* so that the air can freely pass through it, so that no blockage will distort or hinder the sound. There will need to be in the overall make-up of the instrument, in its wood or metal and its design, a givenness to receive, a *receptivity* to the breath, and a *responsiveness* to this breath: a capacity to let it be transformed into sound, to let it flow forth from the instrument and allow for music. Openness, emptiness, receptivity, and response seem essential for a good wind instrument. They are also essential to authentic personhood.

It never ceases to astound me how the wisdom of the ages, particularly as it has been expressed in mystical thought, has spoken to these very characteristics, seeing them as primary in the divine-human encounter to which we are called and for which, as our Christian tradition tells us, we were expressly created: in contemplating Mary's fullness of personhood, Caryll Houselander puts it beautifully:

I am your reed, sweet shepherd, glad to be.
Now, if you will, breathe out your joy in me
And make bright song.
Or fill me with the soft moan of your love
When your delight has failed to call or move
The flock from wrong.

Make children's songs, or any songs to fill
Your reed with breath of life; but at your will
Lay down the flute,
And take repose, while music infinite
Is silence in your heart; and laid on it
Your reed is mute.[1]

Thomas Merton sees us as "a gap, an emptiness" that longs for fulfillment, whose very nature yearns to be "completed by [the one] from whom we come."[2] For Meister Eckhart we are the place where God can pour God's self out. He employs a variety of images to portray our essential emptiness, our receptivity, and our responsiveness. Like Houselander, he sees us as "virgin mothers": "Into our openness, he says, God sends His/Her silent overwhelming presence. We become the *there*, the place, the home for this presence."[3] He likens our personhood to that of a mirror whose very nature (as empty, open, reflecting space) is to give back to the one who gazes into it his or her countenance.

"Eckhart tells us that as virgin souls we are called to be like this mirror: to become the silent place of God's presence so that in our releasement nothing other remains in us. We receive our being from God. Our being is God's presence."[4] Eckhart's foremother, Mechtild of Magdeburg thinks the same thoughts: "When God shines we must reflect," she says, "Each of us is a mirror of eternal contemplation, with a reflection that must surely be that of the living Son of God with all his works."[5] Through our openness—our *there*—our otherness as human can become one with God. "But it is not sufficient to be a virgin soul. A virgin must receive the seed and bear fruit."[6] This is done through gratitude whereby we become aware of the giver and let God flow out from us back to God in praise and thanksgiving. "Gratitude is the movement from the one who receives to the one who gives. It echoes the goodness of the giver and returns to him/her."[7] Angelus Silesius uses similar imagery: "To reflect God in all that is both now and here," he says,

> my heart must be a mirror
> empty,
> bright,
> and clear.[8]

Not only the Christian West, however, speaks of the authenticity of human personhood as emptiness and open receptivity. Lao Tsu exhorts:

Empty yourself of everything.
Let the mind rest at peace.
The ten thousand things rise and fall while the Self
    watches their return.
They grow and flourish and then return to the
    source.
Returning to the source is stillness, which is the
    way of nature.
The way of nature is unchanging.
Knowing constancy is insight.
Not knowing constancy leads to disaster.
Knowing constancy the mind is *open.*
With an open mind you will be openhearted.[9]

The Tao is an empty vessel; it is used but not filled. [10]

The wise therefore rule by emptying hearts.[11]

Frederick Franck, author of *Messenger of the Heart*, links the reflections of Angelus Silesius "with observations by ancient Zen Masters." Franck tells us that:

Reaching spiritual maturity, enlightenment, is to realize Emptiness, Suchness, as the mystery of our very being, as being our very quintessence. It is the moment that the "Structure of Reality" breaks through, that the Indwelling Spirit overcomes the defenses of the ego, and becomes Self-aware in us.[12]

To help explain what he means, he then shares a story well worth repeating here, for it brilliantly parallels Eckhart and Mechtild, as well as Silesius. The story concerns the Empress Wu who lived in China some 1400 years ago. Wu was keenly interested in the Hwa Yen sages who had particular insights concerning the relation "of the One and the Many, of God and his [her] creatures, and of the creatures one to another." Since she could not find the time to read the rather extensive literature on this subject, she asked Fa Tsang (643–712 A.D.), one of the founders of Hwa Yen, to give her a simple explanation:

> Fa Tsang went to work and appointed one of the palace rooms so that eight large mirrors stood at the eight points of the compass. Then he placed two more mirrors, one on the ceiling and one on the floor. A candle was suspended from the ceiling in the center of the room. When the Empress entered, Fa Tsang lit the candle. The Empress cried: "How marvelous! How beautiful."
>
> Fa Tsang pointed at the reflection of the flame in each of the ten mirrors and said: See, Your Majesty: this demonstrates the relationship of the One and the Many, of God to each one of his [her] Creatures. The Empress said: "Yes, indeed, Master! And what is the relationship of each creature to the others?" Fa Tsang answered: Just watch, Your Majesty, how each mirror not only reflects the one flame in the center. Each mirror also reflects the reflections of the flame in all the other mirrors, until an infinite number of flames fills them all. All these reflections are mutually identical; in a sense they are interchangeable, in another sense each one exists individually. This shows the true relationship of each being to its neighbor, to all that is! . . .
>
> Based on this insight is the Kegon term "The Great Compassionate Heart." This Great Compassionate Heart is not some mythical object. It is the quality of awareness that sees all phenomena (including of course oneself) as part of, as rising out of Emptiness; literally remaining this Emptiness while assuming a temporal form, and finally being reabsorbed by Emptiness.[13]

FROM EMPTINESS TO TRANSCENDENCE

Moving from the mystical and the poetic to the more secular and speculative, we find that even in the realm of atheistic humanism the essential emptiness of authentic humanness is upheld. Jean Paul Sartre distinguishes human *consciousness* (what he calls the *pour soi* or "for itself") from the world of *being* (the *en soi* or "in itself") by its fundamental *negativity*. Humanness, for Sartre, is identified by what it lacks. I find myself at all times through my awareness that I am not the other—any other, any thing; that I am no-thing; that I am emptiness. Sartre calls this discovery "nihilation," and sees in it the root of human transcendence.

> Consciousness always says *distance*—not being that of which consciousness is conscious. The compact density of the "in itself" thus is broken by consciousness. In the "in itself" there is no room for negativity [emptiness]: because the "in itself" fully coincides with itself, it is the fullness of being. Only where there is question of consciousness can there be question of negativity. Consciousness is nothing but nihilation. . . .
>
> [T]he being of consciousness is Nothing. The being which makes negativity enter into the world must be its own Nothing.[14]

Sartre's understanding of the human being lays stress on its difference from the world of things. He affirms our uniqueness and resists all reification. For him human subjectivity moves beyond things. By its very nature as emptiness it transcends them. As John Macquarrie, quoting from *Being and Nothingness*, points out: "Human reality is its own surpassing toward what it lacks." Macquarrie adds: "[The human being] is the desire for self-subsisting being, and this means . . . that he [she] is the desire for God."[15] Sartre, of course, rejects the notion of God. His intention is strictly focused on showing that human subjectivity (consciousness) is not a thing. He uses the word, *Neant*, "Nothingness," for this purpose and refuses to attribute to it anything positive. To do so, he claims, would be to reify the human and to live "in bad faith"; to deny subjectivity and reduce the human to an object for investigation, categorization, and identification, thus leading to the ultimate destruction of our freedom-to-become, that is, our transcendence.

It is not our intention here to discuss in greater detail the meaning and validity of Sartre's claim. It is extreme and truly as frustrating as he intended it to be—portraying, as it does, a transcendence leading nowhere, unable to identify any stable direction, to hold on to any-*thing*. For our purposes it is of value only in confirming what seems to be a universal intuition concerning the nature of personhood as emptiness, and to introduce the notion of transcendence as integrally connected with this emptiness. As later, more detailed reflections will reveal, Sartre's view of consciousness can also be helpful to us in expanding our understanding of the beginning of human consciousness which seems to emerge very much along the lines of the process of nihilation described by him, with all its unpleasantness and negativity. In the early phases of his or her consciousness, the youngster's need to separate his or her identity from that of the significant other—a need that is essential for the emergence of self-awareness—is accomplished precisely through the insistence on difference: the "I am not you" syndrome of the "terrible two's" that allows for movement beyond coenesthesis and thus for the establishment of a separate "I." Finding oneself in opposition to others is, of course, not restricted to the two-year-old. Ambition, competition, prejudice and its rejection of the different, all speak most clearly to this phenomenon of human self-understanding. The difference here lies in the fact that during the "terrible two's" one expects "nihilation" as a normal expression of the awakening ego; in later life, on the other hand, it can become an aberration where the other, as Sartre claims, truly is seen as "hell."

For a more positive perspective on the no-thing, the emptiness of human existence that allows for its essential transcendence, Heidegger's view seems much more appropriate. He symbolizes the human person as a clearing in the woods capable, due to its empty space, of receiving the light and letting it shine where trees would otherwise have obscured it. He sees human subjectivity as the place, the *Da*, where being (*Sein*) can appear, and calls it, therefore, *Dasein*.

In human existence "being" and "nothingness" unite. We are being-that-is-transcended. We are movement beyond ourselves and beyond the world of things, even as we recognize and understand ourselves as in the world and concerned with things. Heidegger calls this movement beyond ourselves "no-thingness."

> Heidegger's other-than-being, then, clearly refers to the subject, who makes wonder, asking about the "why" of beings, i.e., science, possible. He calls the subject "non-being" because the subject is not like what he has called (cosmic) being. This non-being, however, is not simply nothing, but something positive, no-thing; a positivity which "lets be" (cosmic) being.[16]

Heidegger's emptiness is the open space where that which is can appear; where meaning can happen, and where being can be shepherded.

> All our heart's courage is the
> echoing response to the
> first call of Being which
> gathers our thinking into the
> play of the world.[17]

Human authenticity, according to Heidegger, calls us to a path of releasement, of giving ourselves over to that which reveals itself in our openness as mystery. Ours is a path of expectancy, of abandonment and waiting—not waiting *for* so much as waiting *upon*, where what we await is left open, thus allowing for revelation. It is a path that necessitates attentiveness, a hearing and responding that is marked by freedom, for it releases into openness all that is. Authentic human openness, therefore, is marked by the creativity of surrender, not of willfulness. Its transcendence lies in its standing beyond *itself* even as it finds itself as being-in-the-world; in its standing beyond *things* even as it gathers them into meaning; in its opening up to the *ground (Being) that*

lets all that is appear (beings, entities, things) although it remains itself
shrouded in mystery.

The essence of the human person, for Heidegger, is found in our
transcendence, "ex-sistence" (Latin, *ex*: out; *sistere*: to stand): "We are
ourselves only, that is, are those who we are, through our pointing into
that which withdraws itself,"[18] that is, into the mystery, the revealing-
with-holding event that Heidegger calls Being.

Once again it is not possible here to discuss extensively the depth
implications of Heidegger's reflections on human transcendence. The
possibilities he opens up for an understanding of faith as intimately
connected with human nature itself are certainly most promising. The
similarity of his thought with the mystical tradition is clearly evident.
Heidegger's attraction to Meister Eckhart is well known, as is the fascination that modern-day scholars, involved with Eastern thought, have
had for Heidegger's writings. For our purposes, we will want to
remember his message most specifically when we probe the significance of human openness and of faith in our adult years. As Sartre
helps us to understand the beginning phases of consciousness,
Heidegger enables us to grasp more thoroughly the meaning of that
empty openness that becomes ever more truly our reality with deepening maturity.

IMMANENT TRANSCENDENCE

At this point it has become necessary, I believe, to contextualize
our reflections on human emptiness and openness somewhat; to ground
them, as it were, in human existentiality. Considerations concerning
the nature of personhood as the place where faith becomes possible
cannot restrict themselves to the realm of transcendence without doing
a serious disservice to the reality of the human condition. Openness in
itself is an abstraction. The hollowness or emptiness of the flute is
found in the wood or the metal that yields to its form. Emptiness does
not of itself produce the flow of sound. It is meaningful only as an
aspect of the instrument that shapes it. The question, therefore, as to
how our human emptiness is contextualized is a necessary one. And

here, once again, Heidegger's thought, though complex in some respects, is helpful.

Although symbolically human emptiness might be compared to a glade, to a mirror, or to an earthen vessel, the empty openness of things is inadequate for our existentiality. Things are ultimately static; we are alive and, though we stand within ourselves, we are also always already beyond ourselves. Our immanence is marked by transcendence; our transcendence, by immanence. We are embodied beings. Our conscious openness is, therefore, intimately connected to our dwelling in time and space, to our historicity, to our being together with others in the world, to the various attunements in which we are held at any given moment, and, most important, to our finitude and our awareness of this—to our "being toward death." These intrinsically human factors modify our receptive responsiveness. They qualify the emptiness that we are. Heidegger calls them "existentials" and sees them as ours by virtue of our humanity as such, that is, not dependent for their being on culture or ethnicity, though their expression is influenced by these and other external circumstances.

Existentials are the ontological given that identifies our openness always as *human* openness. *That they are present* (ontological) is not altered by anything; *how they are present* (ontic) can be altered by various circumstances. To illustrate: My "being toward death" is unchangeable and unpreventable, no matter how well I take care of myself. It will, in one way or another, infiltrate my self-understanding and the meaningfulness of reality generally. I am ontologically finite, and that finitude contextualizes my openness to the world—my existence. However, the actual *way* in which I relate to death, that is, whether I am anxious or at peace, courageous or despairing, will have a lot to do with the experiences of death I have had vicariously. It will also be influenced by my faith, by my upbringing, by my cultural training.

The distinction between the ontological and the ontic character of existentials can be illustrated also with respect to time: My relationship to time, my being temporal, is an ontological fact. It is a given. I cannot even envision existence outside of the threefold dynamic of past, present, and future that I share with all other human beings. Response, however, to this dynamic is individualized. My age, my interest in the events of the moment, my fear of impending events, and many other factors will affect how I see time—whether it appears as fleeting to me, for example, or whether it seems endless; whether I experience it as something that I cannot have enough of, or as something that must be endured. *That I am in time* is a universal human condition. *How I respond to time*—my past and my future now—is uniquely my issue. It is individualized in me.

Human Embodiment

The immanence of human openness is perhaps most readily understood as one meditates on human embodiment and spatiality. Although every human being is to be found, at any given moment, at some particular point in space and is therefore, along with everything else that is, some*where* and, thus, limited—geometrically separated from other beings—the spatiality of personhood *also transcends these boundaries*. The end of a physical object, no matter how sophisticated, is its magnetic field. Closed to the perception of its own presence and to the presence of others, its spatial relation is the short or long distance between it and other objects. Human spatiality, in spite of the object-like appearance of our embodiments, however, is fundamentally different. Medard Boss puts it well:

[N]ot the most modern computer has a world ["Da"] into whose *openness other beings can appear*, reveal themselves, and be *received*. No matter how many or how intense the impulses reaching the energetic field of a computer, it is never *so open* that it can perceive the impulses as such, grasp their significance and respond appropriately to what is understood of them. Whatever is in space as non-living matter is, perceives nothing of its own presence in "space," nor of the presence of other beings, nor of the significance and referential context that constitute the specific character of what is present. . . .

[T]he spatial quality of the human world is in no way comparable to the geometric space in which inanimate, "world-less" objects are present. . . . [T]he spatiality of the human world is *open, unobstructed and clear* to the extent that phenomena may address us through it with their meanings and contexts of reference. . . .

Whatever confronts [the human person] through the openness and clearness of space will inevitably address him [or her] in its significance, owing to the fact that human existence is itself spatial. It is spatial in the sense that the *basic characteristic of its existence is openness and receptivity.* Human presence is in no way confined to the point in space at which the human body (as self-contained physical object) is to be found.[19]

What makes my spatiality human is my potential to be present not only where my physical body is operating, but also and at the same time, where I am headed, or even where I long to be.

[A]s an existing human being, *as* the opening and spanning of a realm by my ability to perceive, I *am* both here and there. I can perceive only what I have already reached or arrived at; how else could I ever have any sense that anything in the world even exists and that it is where it is? How could I desire or approach anything in the realm of my world if I had not already grasped it perceptively and thereby already been with it? . . .

Human existence does not *possess* this openness in the form of one of a number of discrete properties. Rather, it *is* nothing other than being open for perceiving and understanding the things it encounters for what they are, and not for anything else.[20]

Complicated though this discussion may appear at first to the uninitiated reader, common parlance shows us that what has been exposed here is, in fact, taken for granted by most of us. Why else would it make sense to point out to someone with whom we are talking and who is walking beside us but seemingly distracted: "you are not with me today"? or tell a beloved who is leaving on a long and far away trip: "I will be with you"? As person I am an embodied presence. "The borders of my bodyhood coincide with those of my openness to the world."[21] They expand or contract depending on my relationship to this world. Numerous writings in modern-day psychology dealing with body language attest to this fact. The contracted posture of a frightened child about to be struck, the withdrawn bodies of racial minorities in an all-white setting, the slovenly posture of low self-esteem, the prostrate body of someone "lost in prayer," the erect and wide-chested posture of a lyric tenor exploding into song, the expanded tension of a baseball athlete about to steal second base, our own ritual gestures during communal worship, all illustrate our human-embodied spatiality as within and also beyond its own physical boundaries because of its receptivity and responsiveness to the world in which we find ourselves.

Temporality

Nor is our contracted or expanded openness to the world restricted to the context of the present situation. We are at all times permeated by and suffused in time. At any given moment we "body forth" our relationship to the past as well as our projection into the future, not just by virtue of the very real aging process that affects our body—grays our hair and wrinkles our skin, but also because of the temporality in which we are held, responding as we do to its threefold modality with varying degrees of emphasis.

Time is not something we *have* like one owns a car. Nor are we ever strictly speaking *in* time, like passengers seated in a bus—successively. Rather, we *dwell* in time, expectant of what is to come (future), aware of what is present, and retentive of what has been (past), with ever alternating shades of attention. The distraught woman crouched on her bed rocking herself to calmness, clutching a pillow for security, may very well be back in her infant years of terror and fear of a threatening grown-up. The world of therapy is perhaps one of the most telling proofs of the distinctly human dynamic of time. Freud's notions of transference and countertransference are rooted, whether he knew it or not, precisely in his brilliant intuition in this regard. Our past, at any moment, can impinge upon, if not engulf, our present and distort our future. Therapy liberates our future by restoring past relationships to a healthier now.

We do not, of course, need to restrict our examples of the ever shifting energies held in the modes of our temporality to therapeutic encounters. The liberated prisoner of war who still trembles at the sight of army boots is back in the camp of many months ago, reliving torturous moments. The agitated patient who cannot sleep the night before surgery is already in the operating room. The mother who weeps at her son's wedding may, even then, be facing future pain. Our body is wrapped up in temporalizing. We weep, we tremble, we cringe, we expand and celebrate in the face of its truth for us. All authentically religious acts speak to this fact. The liturgical celebration of the death and the resurrection of the Christ, as this event lives itself anew in each and everyone of us, is a clear illustration of our acknowledgment, conscious or not, of human transcendence and its relation to time and space. We bear within us even now the passion and the glory of the Christ toward the transformation, the Christification, of the universe. In authentic ritual *we proclaim the reality of our past as our future here and now*. We are held in the event and stand out (ex-sist) in openness toward it.

Coexistence

Religious acts speak equally eloquently to humanness as essentially communal. Our existence is always coexistence. We dwell in time-space relationship *together with others in the world*. Here we must stress once more, as Medard Boss does, that it is not

enough to interpret human *co*existence simply as the appearance, "here" and "here," of physical human bodies. The person walking toward me might be thinking just now of a friend
in San Francisco, and as long as he [she] does, he [she] is over
"there," his [her] whole existing absorbed in this relationship
to his [her] friend in such a way that he [she] extends far
beyond the observable volume of his [her] body.[22]

Human coexistence stretches far beyond concrete spatial proximi-
ty and the immediate "now" of time. Statements praising "real togetherness," observations about someone as being "distant," as not being
"with us," or "one with us," attest to our awareness of this.

The fundamental trait of the existential coexistence of human
beings appears in their jointly sustaining and maintaining the
openness of the world they clear in common. It is carried out
in shared ways of perceiving and responding to whatever is
commonly encountered.[23]

Once again, the importance of this existential reality with respect to
worship and ritual should be obvious. Lack of enthusiasm and real
meaningfulness in this area can easily be traced to failure in maintaining openness to a *common world*. Worship is more than *attending*
church services. It is more than communion counts. Because of its
communal nature, it speaks eloquently of the depth of coexistence. Its
perversion lies precisely in turning its coexistential reality into a per-
formance, a "one-man show."

Our coexistence is ours in our very essence. Our being is marked
by togetherness with others. In the strictest sense, humans are really
never alone. Conceived of a communal love act, we were nurtured
within another, brought forth and empowered toward consciousness by
our parents. Thus, when we reached self-awareness and conscious
reflective capacity, we already found ourselves with a past—our history was already in the making. "[W]e find ourselves," as James J. Bacik
borrowing from Heidegger puts it, "thrown into a world both of per-

sons and things which have a power to shape our consciousness and determine our existence";[24] and have, in fact, done both before we were ever aware of it.

Already our most primitive consciousness carries communal awareness. We see through the eyes of others so that even our most original thoughts are really, in the deepest sense, at all times co-original. Our vision is ever co-vision. We stand on the shoulders of our ancestors. Our heritage permeates us, and our self-awareness is touched by coexistence. For better or worse, we see ourselves reflected in the eyes of others—an insight captured well in the healing "ministry" of Carl Rogers's "unconditional positive regard."

Coexistent openness is, of course, constituted in the dynamic of receptivity and response. Our primordial co-being does not excuse us from the responsibility for our destiny. Though heredity and environment shape our vision, we are *at the end* of total determinism. Our response, therefore, calls us to creativity. It reveals itself paradoxically, if you will, as surrender permeated with freedom. Bacik puts it well in what might be considered a brief summary on the nature of existential openness:

> [W]e are called upon to create our world, to use our time constructively, and to influence history. In all of this process we cannot escape the limitation implied in our creaturehood, our bodiliness, and our immersion in the rhythm of time. Our situation in life is always influencing and limiting our free disposal of ourselves. Any effort to live in total self-sufficiency or in a pure subjective interiority can only lead to frustration.[25]

Our surrender, then, is to the facticity of our creaturehood. It involves recognition of boundaries, of extraneous influences, of physical, social, psychological constraints. The freedom of surrender lies in our creative response to our fundamental reality, in our genuine resourcefulness, in our vision, in our courageous *yes* to life lived fully. "Despite all determinisms in life," says James J. Bacik, "human beings

have the power to take up an attitude toward themselves and thus to
assume responsibility for the totality of their existence."[26] This is our
freedom.

"Being toward Death"

Perhaps our creaturehood and our lack of self-sufficiency come to
the fore most poignantly when we are faced with our ultimate finitude.
What Heidegger calls our "being toward death" confronts human existence as an ontological given. It is part of the very texture of our living—right from our beginning, deep in our mother's womb, until our
final breath. Experiments in psycholytic therapy attest to this fact with
amazing accuracy. June Singer, commenting on Stanislav Grof's therapeutic work in the area of birth trauma, discusses reexperiencing birth
as follows:

> What is particularly interesting is that in reexperiencing the
> birth process, the individual undergoes sensations not only of
> birth, but *also of death*. A new philosophical awareness may
> emerge from this experience, as the person realizes the frailty
> of the individual and the impermanence of the individual's
> life relative to the larger course of Life itself. *The realization*
> *that one must leave the world exactly as one came into it,*
> *bereft of everything one has acquired during a lifetime, points*
> *up the similarity between birth and death: birth is not only a*
> *beginning of life in this world, it is also a death to the world*
> *from which the infant issues—the womb-world—which is*
> *nourished by the seed of the generations.*[27]

The "new philosophical awareness" identified here by Singer is, of
course, new only in the area of contemporary scientific research. In
actuality, it is as ancient as philosophy itself. The early Greeks were so
imbued with it that they identified human existence as a whole by it,
calling themselves "mortals."

Death, and the birth to which it opens up right from our beginning, is the archetype, if you will, of our existence. The birth-death dynamic is our story. By it we identify meaning and significance. It is not surprising, therefore, that our deepest religious impulses are charged with it. The "Charter Event" of Christianity in this regard is the most profound example: Is not the death and the resurrection of Christ Jesus a bodying forth, a living out, yes, most truly, a redeeming of this dynamic? Perhaps the primacy of the death and resurrection of the God-man ought to be seen and understood not so much in the historical event of Jesus' passion, as in the human condition itself (dying, being born; dying and being born once again), which from primordial times has needed and has called for healing, for Christification. Christ, after all, came to show us how to be fully human, and death, in its deepest significance, is part of that.

"Death," says Medard Boss, "is the unsurpassable limit of human existence."[28] At one and the same time, it restricts and expands our openness to meaning, because in the face of its absolute certainty every possibility needs to be evaluated.

> Death, in one sense destructive, is in another sense creative of unified, responsible selfhood, the concerns of which become ordered in the face of the end. Furthermore, death also becomes a criterion for judging our concerns. Death exposes the superficiality and triviality of many of the ambitions and aspirations on which [we] spend [our] energies. What Heidegger calls "everyday" existence is frequently the escape from responsibility, the covering up of death and finitude, the jumping from one immediate concern to the next without any thought that our existence, as bounded, has the potentiality for some measure of unity and wholeness. . . . [T]he fact of death makes clear . . . the transient and nugatory character of the achievements of the [one] who does not take into account the full range of possibility and facticity.[29]

The mark of transcendence is clearly visible here in the very depths of the human condition. We are, as it were, gathered in by our finitude and, in this experience, point beyond ourselves. Recognition and acceptance of our transience and mortality bring with them the re-collection of oneself toward meaningful possibilities. "Gaining the whole world" ceases to be the issue, as our finitude highlights for us the essentials of life. Medard Boss puts it well:

> Each *Da-sein* dies its own death in total loneliness. The consequence of this insight is by no means a resigned, passive fixation on what must happen sooner or later. On the contrary, in accepting mortality as [our] most characteristic, final, isolated, and—except for the actual moment of death—certain existential possibility, [we] first realize [our] responsibility for every instant of [our] existence. If [we] were not finite and mortal, [we] would never miss anything. There would always be time to catch up and make something good. But for someone who is mortal, no situation happens twice in quite the same way. If what [we do] is not in tune with the moment, that moment is irrevocably lost to [us]; [our] conscience will remind [us] that [we have] fallen behind in fulfilling [our] existence.[30]

It is clear that death as "an essential trait of existence" and, thus, as a foundational modification of our openness, marks our "ceasing to be" as fundamentally different from other finite beings. "[P]lants and animals do not *die*, as human beings do. They simply perish."[31] Death is "the most thoroughly pervasive and peculiarly human trait of all."[32] The openness to meaning that it makes possible for us frees us from absorption in, and surrender to, everyday-ness. Knowing that "we do not have here a lasting city" (Heb 13:14) frees us from the control of "things" and returns us to ourselves, brings us home to the no-thing-ness where, paradoxically, we find fulfillment.

Our death, then, is never a merely biological event that befalls us at some unknown moment in history. It is, as Bacik sees it, at all times also a "spiritual act," whereby we hand ourselves over: "[D]eath is not just the separating of body and soul, but our great opportunity to ratify the general orientation of our lives toward the good and thus to reach our final fulfillment."[33]

Understood this way, our being toward death carries within it a profound call to faith. Death marks most clearly our being as transcendent, for through it, as Rahner would have us see, we are opened up to radical freedom: "In death the whole life of a person is finalized, fulfilled, and brought into the presence of God."[34] Our being toward death orients our entire life in the direction of choice for or against ultimate value; for or against God. Human death, for Rahner, receives its deepest significance only in the death of Christ. We have touched on this already somewhat. Suffice it to say here simply that Rahner insists that "the whole of Christ's life [as, indeed, the whole of our lives also] must be viewed from the perspective of his death. In his death, Christ summed up in a definitive act the totality of his person and his freedom,"[35] and thus transformed, Christified, human dying once and for all.

Attunement

In a later chapter, our considerations concerning the meaning of grace and God's compassionate reaching out toward us will lead us to the "supernatural existential" (Karl Rahner) and will once more invite us to reflect on the modalities of human openness. The present discussion, however, on the existentials and on our immanent transcendence would not be complete without at least some brief reference to what Heidegger calls *Gestimmtheit*,[36] generally translated as "attunement" or "mood." Human openness, receptivity, and response both to itself as well as to the entire world of reality is permeated at all times with some disposition or other. Being attuned, in other words, *is* the way human beings are open. There is "no such thing as an initially unattuned existence in which a disposition of some kind [happiness, equanimity, anxiety, for example] simply arises now and then through the intrusion of some internal or external cause."[37]

Furthermore, human openness is potentially every attunement or mood of which persons are capable. We are innately (ontologically) disposed to attunement, which, in its turn, permeates and influences our perceptive openness with its particular color and flavor.

> Every attunement *as* attunement is a particular mode of the perceptive openness of our existence. The prevailing attunement is at any given time the condition of our openness for perceiving and dealing with what we encounter; the pitch at which our existence, as a set of relationships to objects, ourselves and other people, is vibrating. What we call moods, feelings, affects, emotions, and states are the concrete modes in which the possibilities for being open are fulfilled. They are at the same time the modes in which this perceptive openness can be narrowed, distorted, or closed off.[38]

It is impossible to discuss in detail here the various moods toward which human existence is disposed. Of significance for our reflection is the recognition that our openness is permeated by them. Just like an instrument, even if out of tune, nevertheless gives forth tone and is, therefore, though in a distorted fashion, "tuned" and in potency toward having its tone adjusted, so human existence is an openness tuned at all times toward all the moods available to humanness. Total "objectivity," therefore, as the contemporary mind would envision it, is illusion. Even a person neutral to a situation will bring his or her own attunement to it and see issues accordingly.

Strange as these observations may appear to someone who has never considered them, it is remarkable how our everyday interactions nevertheless reflect our awareness of them. The mood of an employer is very much on the mind of his or her secretary when openness to a request is being considered. Nor ought the secretary's caution necessarily be considered as manipulative. It is utterly valid and reasonable to consider attunement in evaluating openness. How often do we decide to "sleep on" an issue before making decisions? Though other existentials, such as embodiment, are involved here, attunement plays a serious role in proper discernment. When in a course on the psychology and spirituality of midlife I recommend that persons in the throes of a crisis postpone all major life decisions, the anxiety, depression, discouragement, and boredom of this crisis, and their effects on a person's openness are very clearly on my mind. Communal gatherings, celebrations, and rituals all reflect our awareness of attunement. Vestments, gestures, music, dance, and decorations in all liturgical settings vary according to the mood that is being expressed. Lack of consideration here directly affects the openness and receptivity of those participating. Consideration regarding attunement, therefore, is essential to public worship.

TRANSCENDENCE AND FREEDOM

Though, for the sake of clarity, we have in this discussion reflected on the various existentials separately, it must be stressed that the ontological modifications of human openness to meaning are really equally primordial. "Every single human phenomenon, no matter how trifling, is inherently constituted of every one of these characteristics,"[39] though one or the other can at any given moment predominate. They merge with each other, overlap and interpenetrate each other. Our embodiment, our being in the world, our spatiality, for example, are clearly all intimately intertwined; as are embodiment and death; time, historicity, and death; time and space; time, space, and coexistence. The existentials belong to the openness that *is* human existence. All of them as interconnected and also with varying degrees of intensity are "of the nature of an ability that allows the meaningfulness of what [a human being] encounters to disclose itself *as* what it is."[40]

Here it may be necessary, once again, to reiterate with Medard Boss that human emptiness and openness

> may not be reified and so misunderstood as a kind of hollow space into which beings may fall, be present, and be stored. . . . As the open realm of perception which it is, human existence is "merely" a realm of fundamental perceptive responsiveness *to* the phenomena of the world. That is why our world can never

be divided into openness of human existence on the one hand
and the totality of concrete nonhuman beings on the other.[41]

The dualistic split between the subjective and the objective world is at
best an abstraction. It simply does not fit the concrete human condition. As human beings we are never totally separated from, but at all
times in relational connection with, the phenomena that light up for us.

Thanks to [our] existential openness to any presence that
reveals itself to [us], [we are] able to allow whatever appears
in the realm of [our] perception simply to be. This allowing
does not mean benign neglect or indifference. It means entering into a relationship to that thing in a way that permits it to
fully evolve its particular meaningfulness.[42]

Human truth emerges in this process as the interplay between *"lighting
up for"* and *"being received and responded to"* within the creative finitude of our openness. Human truth, therefore, is never total and
absolute. It is held in the event of what Heidegger calls "unconcealing-
concealment."[43] It is, even at its clearest, pervaded by mystery, and our
surrender to this fact is what, in its deepest sense, constitutes our freedom.[44]

For those who see freedom merely as a choice between alterna-
tives; as the nonrestricted ability to do or not do as one pleases; or even
as the readiness to do what is demanded of one, as the willingness to
comply to the necessary, the suggestion that a more fundamental
understanding of freedom would describe it as an "open surrender to
the mystery," might be quite confusing. It identifies freedom primarily
as an involvement, a participation in a process, a disposition of readiness, rather than, first and foremost, the power to choose. Although it
does not deny the power to choose, it sees involvement as a precondition for it. Freedom is essentially a state of being. We *are* free. We do
not *have* freedom as a property. It may even be more correct to say that
freedom "has us." We are held, if you will, by our very transcendent
openness in a process of revelation that allows for truth to emerge and

the world to unfold in the eternal interplay between clarity and obscurity; between disclosure and withdrawal, once again, into mystery.

It seems to me that the religious archetype for this understanding of freedom as an essential mode of our very being is, above all, Mary, the Mother of God—the "reed of God." Her fiat was the very surrender to the unfathomable that in its very lighting up remained, nevertheless, shrouded in mystery. Mary's "yes" was made possible by the freedom in which she was held. Her being *as surrendered*, if you will, was the precondition for the act of consent. In a deeper than biological sense, she was Mother (the virgin mother of the mystics we meditated on earlier) *before* the spoken fiat; and, because she was who she was, the Mystery could unfold in her consent and become fruit.

It is clear that reflection upon this interpretation of freedom reveals it as having profound ethical implications. As we have already discussed in the previous chapter, ours is an age of speculative thought—of truth as clarity and certainty. Ethics, too, is frequently viewed as a moral science that deals with the measurable and definable. Understood, however, within the context of human freedom as we have meditated here, ethics would be seen more foundationally as, first and foremost, our abode—according to the original Greek meaning of *ethos*: dwelling place. "*Ethos*," according to Bernard J. Boelen, "is the behavior we *are*, the behavior in response to the call of our own authentic being."[45] Our being, however, is freedom, surrender to the mystery. It cannot be imprisoned in objective certainty, in abstraction, in dogmatism. It belongs to the noncalculable, the undefinable, the domain of reverential listening and openness. We are more than a formula, more than a deduction or verifiable quantity. Therefore, we are ethical in the most profound sense when we dwell within the integrity of our being as light permeated with darkness, as truth in which mystery prevails—as truth, in fact, made whole by *the* Mystery.

Our forgetfulness of this, brings thoughtlessness and disintegration—the idolatry, as it were, of things in their thingness, that is, things not held in and sustained by the mystery of no-thingness and, therefore, given much too much power—possessing us, if you will, and thus bringing about sin.

A classic example, to clarify the above, is given by Erich Neumann in *Depth Psychology and a New Ethic*. He calls it the *idee fixe*,[46] that forces the individual or group to ignore essential aspects of reality (i.e., its inherent mystery and its often seemingly paradoxical self-revelation, its inherence in the no-thing). Because these aspects are ignored, distortion ensues. Neumann suggests that, "every form of fanaticism, every dogma and every type of compulsive one-sidedness is finally overthrown by precisely those elements which it has itself repressed, suppressed or ignored."[47]

What Neumann cites as one form of *idee fixe* is ego inflation. It is dangerous not because the value proclaimed, the particular person, for example, stuck in the inflation, is unworthy of attention, but rather because "the limited individual loses contact with his [her] own limitations and becomes inhuman."[48] The ancients called this *hubris* (pride), and exemplified its disastrous effects in the myth of Icarus. He *had* to fall, for he soared too high.[49] In modern times we have variations of Icarus, as Neumann points out:

> The positivist belief in progress was one of the precursors of the First World War, and the arrogation of modern man [woman], regarding himself [herself] as the meaning and evolutionary culmination of creation, was a prelude to the bestial arrogation of the Aryan *Herrenvolk* under National Socialism.[50]

Any kind of absolutism invites similar distortions, perhaps not always as disastrous, but, nevertheless, equally untrue and illusory. If human truth does not hold itself in the acknowledgment of its essential limitations, it becomes pseudo-truth, and no law or sacred proclamation will grant it immunity from its own distortions.

Interestingly enough, the denial of our limitations brings with it a crippling of our transcendence as well:

> The uniqueness and individuality of [the human person] is realised precisely by the self-differentiation of the creaturely and limited from the unlimited power of the Creator. In infla-

tion, this basic situation is by-passed, and [the human being] becomes a chimera, a "pure spirit" or disembodied ghost.[51]

The sins of "disembodied ghosts" in the Christian West abound: Truth that does not accept its own boundaries, hence, the possibility of inherent "untruth," dwells in falsehood. It enslaves itself to its own absolutes and betrays the freedom in which it is held. And what are the sins of disembodied ghosts? They are the denial of human facticity— the rejection of situation—of the particular human story. They are blind to

> all the "givens" of any particular existence—intelligence, race, temperament, and many other factors that no one chooses for himself [herself]. Environment and heredity, our place in history and society, these contribute so much to making us what we are that the area of the possible is cut down, sometimes, it would seem, almost to vanishing point. Every freedom is balanced against limitation, perhaps a limitation of power that prevents us from carrying out a policy, or perhaps a limitation of knowledge that frustrates our intention. So existence is always characterized by the *tension between possibility and facticity*, between [our] freedom and [our] manifold finitude.[52]

To ignore this is to lay impossible burdens both on oneself and others; to flee from the immanence in our transcendence; to blind oneself to the irrational in our rationality, to the impotence that often fetters our sense of obligation and responsibility; and, ultimately, and in the extreme to which unfortunately modern times are not immune, to succumb to a blind form of angelism that often, and paradoxically, expresses itself in the lowest forms of irrationality, brutality, and animality imaginable. The tortures of the Inquisition, witch hunts, mass exterminations for the sake of pure blood, computerized bombing of military targets that kills thousands "cleanly" and "efficiently" by destroying all life-support systems for them, medical experimentation upon aborted fetuses and syphilitic prisoners, are but a few examples of disembodied brutality.

Depth psychology has in our times, of course, done much to assist us toward holding ourselves more realistically in the tension between possibility and facticity: transcendence and immanence. Whether we remember Freud's "id," Erich Fromm's "archaic nature," or Jung's "collective and personal shadow," the message is clear: ignoring our immanence leads to disaster. Growth, maturation, and wholeness are possible only in the creative tension between the polarities of our existence. Letting either of them go invariably results in personal and/or social disintegration.

Authentic human freedom as dwelling in the integrity of our surrender to the mystery, then, is anything but a simple decision. Surrender, here, is not passive acquiescence to the inevitable—a kind of fatalism to which we bow in deterministic resignation. Freedom is acceptance of call. It is courage in the deepest sense of the word. It is a dynamic process of becoming ever more fully who we are.

CONCLUSION

The preceding pages have undoubtedly proved somewhat difficult reading for anyone not previously acquainted with the language and concepts of existential thought—be it in the area of philosophy, psychology, or theology. I have presented these somewhat complex reflections, however, in the hope of providing what I believe to be a necessary, holistic perspective that needs to replace the generally dualistic view of personhood and consequent faith interpretation still prevalent among some contemporary theologians, as well as among ordinary believers whose faith instruction largely comes from parish life where, sadly, theological reflection has often remained in a pre–Vatican II limbo.

If James Bacik is right, and the experience of self is the experience of God,[53] then the anthropological starting point in the divine-human encounter must be considered with great care and deliberation. We have reflected extensively, therefore, throughout these pages on the significance of our personhood; on the meaning of inherent emptiness and the call within our very being to openness and transcendence. We have tried to contextualize the open receptivity and response that we *are* within the parameters of our humanness, and have attempted to understand human freedom in this light. Our task now is to concretize these foundational reflections. We hope to do this by exploring in greater detail human growth and maturation as such. Bernard J. Boelen sees human development as freedom engaged "in the process of freeing itself." We might wish to add: It is movement into openness, widening out to ever greater receptivity and response. It is consciousness becoming ever more truly conscious.

Our primary concern in the succeeding pages will be not only to understand the process of human maturation, but more specifically to relate it to our movement into God, thus gaining an ever deeper understanding into the possibility of faith. Ultimately human maturation, and healing, and wholeness, and holiness are all one. What this means in the concrete is our immediate concern.

3

The Risk of Being Human

What we call the beginning is often the end
And to make an end is to make a beginning.
The end is where we start from. . . .

We shall not cease from exploration
And the end of all our exploring
Will be to arrive where we started
And know the place for the first time.

(T. S. Eliot "Little Gidding")

The "dynamic process of becoming ever more fully who we are" as
conscious openness in the face of mystery is, indeed, an exploration, a
journey into freedom. In lectures on maturation I frequently refer to it
as a coming forth from the Heart of God and, ultimately, a return to
this Heart in what T. S. Eliot would describe as:

A condition of complete simplicity
(Costing not less than everything)

("Little Gidding")

The story is told by Chogyam Trungpa in his book, *Born in Tibet*,
of a very saintly old man in north-east Tibet whose life had been filled
with compassion and concern for others in need, especially for the very
poor. As he was approaching death, he made one last and very simple
request of his family. He asked that after his death his body be left

undisturbed for a week, and that only then the necessary funeral rites be celebrated. "Soon," so Trungpa tells us, "he did die; and his body, wrapped in old clothes, was carried into a small room. The corpse-bearers noted that though the old man had been tall the body already appeared to have grown smaller." It seemed to get smaller and smaller as the days progressed until, on the eighth day—the day designated for burial—it had completely disappeared. "Everyone, of course, was astounded. But when the family reported the event to a learned local lama, the learned man told them that a similar happening had been reported several times in the past: the body of the saintly man had been absorbed into the Light."[1]

A story such as this puzzles us. Life is too mundane, too concerned with everyday matters, for many of us to comprehend such total "absorption." Yet unless we resign ourselves complacently to the fact that our mystery too has eclipsed,[2] we need to come to understand this *being taken into the Light* as the all-consuming quest of our life's longing, as the culmination of our self-emptying, as our homecoming into God's heart:

> And all shall be well and
> All manner of things shall be well
> When the tongues of flame are in-folded
> Into the crowned knot of fire
> And the fire and the rose are one.

("Little Gidding")

GROWTH INTO ONENESS

At-onement is the story of our life. It is the single most significant reason for our existence. Our yearning for it, consciously or not, takes on the multifaceted, joy-filled, as well as agonizing dimensions of life identified as the "human condition." It is, as Eliot assures us, completely simple, and, at the same time, it costs us everything.

There are numerous developmental theories identifying the human passage into at-onement. Not all see it within a religious context *per se*. All, however, recognize it as depth actualization, as maturation, as movement into wisdom, into insight—as becoming whole. It is not my intention here to expose in detail any one particular theory over another, although the thoughtful approach to human maturation developed by Bernard J. Boelen seems most suited for a foundational understanding of our human "openness in process"—of freedom involved in the process of freeing itself[3]—and will, therefore, be referred to more frequently and exposed in greater depth.

As I mentioned, the aim of these reflections is to further contextualize the faith journey—to see how the openness, the emptiness that we are, widens and hollows out throughout our lifetime, and readies itself in ever deeper ways for the breakthrough of God. It is clear that the openness of an infant cannot be seen in the same manner as that of an aged grandmother or grandfather. It ought to be equally clear that, although we are baptized in infancy, our faith at that time in no way compares to that of a more mature person. As our openness widens, so does our response to the holy, and, although the wisdom of mature insight reveals to us many years later that "nothing can separate us from the love of God" (Rom 8:35–39), the conscious experience of this takes much living.

Boelen broadly identifies three levels of human openness, maturation, human receptivity and response to reality. He sees each of these levels nuanced by numerous sublevels and suggests that movement from awareness to greater awareness is frequently accompanied by periods of crisis: intensely experienced turning points in our way of seeing and appreciating both ourselves and the world around us.

LEVEL I

The biological level of awareness, what Boelen identifies as the "bodily" level, holds the human being roughly between conception and the period of ego emergence. The latter is chronologically situated somewhere around two years of age and often referred to as the "terrible two's." The tendency prevails even today to interpret the biological level of awareness from an adult perspective and, therefore, to minimize its actual impact on later adult life with its obviously greater

sophistication of consciousness. Fetal psychology, however, and especially the work in psycholytic therapy pioneered by Stanislav Grof
(Czechoslovakia and later the USA) and by clinical theologian Frank
Lake (England), attest to the fact that the "realms of the human uncon-
scious" and, one might add, of human experience in general, are much
wider than previously held, and extend, in fact, to the very beginnings
of human life itself.

Blastocystic Bliss—"Unearned Mysticism"

Grof's work centered primarily on the last trimester of fetal life
and on the birth process itself.[4] Lake, on the other hand, investigated
the period immediately following conception and the first trimester of
life.[5] There he discovered, prior to all moments of distress and terror
not uncommon in the womb, a time that he identified as "sheer bliss,"
a period of "free-floating wonder, free of attachment of any kind."
Lake called this experience (reported by at least one out of every three
persons engaged in psycholytic therapy) "blastocystic bliss," envelop-
ing the fertilized egg as it travels down the Fallopian tube toward the
womb:

> The blastocyst is self-subsistent, since it has no attachment.
> There is no time, no space, no light, no dark, no right, no left,
> no up, no down, no masculine, no feminine—only experien-
> tial wonderment in a completely monistic state. It is as though
> "I encompass the whole universe. It is I and I am it."[6]

In my lectures on this topic I frequently refer to these bliss-filled
moments of our beginning as the "period of unearned mysticism." This
designation is quite in line with the findings of both Grof and Lake,
who in their probings into the prenatal experiences of human existence
became acutely aware that the biological and the spiritual aspects of
life are really inseparable: "[T]he barrier between consciousness and
the sacral dimension of life disappears. . . . As the person returns in
awareness to the biological matrix, its spiritual dimension reveals

itself; so the pre-personal and the trans-personal experiences are blended,"[7] and all is seen as holy.

These very early moments of blastocystic "mysticism" seem to be experiences of oneness that are totally gratuitous. I have often wondered whether perhaps they are given to us at the beginning of life as a foretaste, so to speak, as a preview of what is to come when we, as human free agents, will have finally grown into full maturity, and there can say our own "yes" to the All:

> We are all able, at the transpersonal stage, to *see life whole.*
> No longer do we limit our seeing to the fragments of self and
> others as isolated entities capable of autonomy or self-suffi-
> ciency. No longer do we regard power as a magic wand, a
> great manipulator that humans can use to achieve superiority
> over others who are less powerful. We begin to understand
> what it means to say, "We are all One." It is an affirmation of
> the union between the divine and the human principles, a
> union which exists on a *profound* and *basic* level and *under-
> lies every plurality* that exists on the level of manifestation.
> The transpersonal perspective allows us to remember that
> Great Knowledge exists, that it is ever-present as an overrid-
> ing consciousness in which we are contained, even while we
> make our peace with the world of small knowledge, of multi-
> plicity.[8]

Joseph Campbell identifies this "Great Knowledge" with Aldous Huxley's "Mind at Large,"[9] and sees it as the ultimate locus of wisdom toward which we all move, and in which, simultaneously, we are held—in which all is held and from which all issues forth. To illustrate this, Campbell cites the Gnostic *Gospel According to Thomas*:

> Whoever drinks from my mouth shall become as I am and I
> myself will become he [she], and the hidden things shall be
> revealed to him [her]. . . . I am the All, the All came forth

from me and the All attained to me. Cleave a piece of wood, I am there; lift up the stone and you will find me there.[10]

The archetype for this transpersonal wisdom, as Jung sees it, is the Self, the depth dimension of the psyche, the Holy Grail of individuation, our life's quest that paradoxically is, nevertheless, ever with us, beckoning us into authentic union and allowing us ultimately "to experience the flow of the energies of the universe in and through our own beings."[11] The Self that blissfully touches us at the beginning and then gently withholds itself once again, awaiting our free embrace, speaks to us of universal openness to the cosmic. It is spirit to whom all things are opened, who becomes all things. It is "child" to whom we must ultimately return if the reign of God is to be ours. "Unearned mysticism," it would seem, is ours at the beginning primarily for the enticing. It is the luring of love, if you will, and presents us with the *leitmotif* for our yearning throughout life.

Encountering the Other

Somewhere around the tenth day after conception the experience of the "other" brings "blastocystic bliss" to an abrupt end. This takes place when the zygote connects with the lining of the mother's womb. The reexperiencing of the first encounter with other-ness through regressive therapy helps the subject recognize "whether the union was an event from which the individual is fleeing, or a state to which he or she aspires to return."[12] Difficult as it may be for some of us to admit, especially in the light of our culture's denial of significance to the fetus, the mother's feeling's about herself and about life in general seem to affect her child even before she knows that she is pregnant. June Singer puts it unambiguously:

The mother's general responses to her own life situation *before* she knew she was pregnant appear to be "discovered" as the subjects relive what comes through to them from their first contact with the womb. The image that the mother has of herself, her sensations, her movements, her anxiety level, can be recognized as having affected the fetus. During the primal integration (the reliving [of pre-natal experiences by the subject undergoing psycholytic therapy]) the strong change in the mother on her discovery of pregnancy may take the form of fetal response to maternal delight or maternal distress. The fetus experiences the mother's affect as it is chemically transmitted through the umbilical cord. If this affect is positive, in the form of attention-giving emotional regard, the fetus develops a feeling of comfortable skin, which may be the basis of later self-esteem and feeling of personal value. But if the fetus receives negative affect, it cannot as easily thrive. It wishes to feel its presence recognized. When this is denied, the ground is set for the anticipation of being disregarded, hence of being of no interest or account in the world.[13]

It is not clear, of course, how much of adult emotional trauma is traceable to such early beginnings as we are discussing here. Trauma, as we all know, can occur throughout our life and can profoundly affect our future. How a person responds to trauma, however, and "how the person interacts with the environment, tends to be a variation on an earlier way of responding."[14] We know today that this "earlier way of responding" can indeed be *very early*, and our knowledge increases our responsibility.

Research much less controversial than the work of Grof and Lake attests to the fact that human intrauterine bonding sets the pattern for bonding between mother and child after birth. "What happens after birth," Thomas Verny, M.D., assures us, "is an elaboration of, and depends on, what happened prior to it."[15] In his book *The Secret Life of the Unborn Child*, he cites numerous examples from fetal psychology, hypnotherapy, and neurological research to illustrate this observation.[16] One example is particularly poignant in this regard and well worth our reflection:

Everything had begun fine, Peter said. [The reference here is to Dr. Peter Fedor-Freybergh, professor of obstetrics and gynecology at the University of Uppsala in Sweden.] At birth, Kristina was robust and healthy. Then something strange happened. Bonding babies invariably move toward the maternal breast, but inexplicably, Kristina didn't. Each time her mother's breast was offered, she turned her head away. At first, Peter thought she might be ill, but when Kristina devoured a bottle of formula milk in the nursery later, he decided her reaction was a temporary aberration. It wasn't. The next day, when Kristina was brought to her mother's room, she refused her breast again; the same thing happened for several days thereafter.

Concerned, but also curious, Peter devised a clever experiment. He told another patient of his about Kristina's baffling behavior and that woman agreed to try breast-feeding the child. When a sleepy Kristina was placed in her arms by a nurse, instead of spurning the woman's breast as she had her mother's, Kristina grasped it and began sucking for all she was worth. Surprised by her reaction, Peter visited with Kristina's mother the next day and told her what had happened. "Why do you suppose the child reacted that way?" he asked. The woman said she didn't know. "Was there an illness during her pregnancy, perhaps?" he suggested. "No, none," she replied. Peter then asked, point blank, "Well, did you want to get pregnant, then?" The woman looked at him and said, "No, I didn't, I wanted an abortion. My husband wanted the child. That's why I had her."

That was news to Peter but, obviously, not to Kristina. She had been painfully aware of her mother's rejection for a long time. She refused to bond with her mother after birth because her mother had refused to bond with her before it. Kristina had been shut out emotionally in the womb and now, though barely four days old, she was determined to protect herself from her mother in any way she could.[17]

The Crisis of Birth

The crisis most significant for this biological level of awareness (Level I) and, indeed, for the rest of human emergence into openness, is that of birth. In the preceding chapter we touched briefly upon the profound connection of birth even with death. We can say at this point that the former is held in the latter even as the latter is pulled toward the former. "There is no moment during [our] lifelong process of birth in which the end is 'not there yet,' " says Bernard Boelen. As fundamental openness to meaning, we do not "move away from [our] beginning, [we move] towards it. [Our] life stretches itself along towards its own birth."[18] This insight appears to be particularly acute for those involved in prenatal and natal therapy. It seems more obvious when one has been enabled to relive one's preconscious or repressed experiences, that "the human process of birth is all of one piece—from the physical separation from the womb and the birth of the biological organism to the birth of the psychological personality and the emergence of authentic ex-sistence. . . . the entire process of human life is essentially a process of birth."[19] It becomes clear, then, why depth events throughout our life so frequently take on the symbolism of birth.

What is of particular interest, furthermore, is that the sacral dimension that has revealed itself as inseparable from the biological matrix permeates our life events as well and, in many cases, is recognized in them without any conscious reference on our part to the experiences of birth that are archetypal of them. Grof identifies four Basic Perinatal Matrices (BPMs) all of which are charged with their own unique spiritual dimension.

We have already discussed the stage of uterine existence (BPM I). Grof—who, as we suggested, did not study this time as far back into its beginning as did Lake—described this time as one of symbiotic unity, "of feelings of security, protection, satisfaction and even cosmic unity, though occasionally 'bad womb' associations occur."[20] Perhaps no one identifies the birth crisis (BPM II, III, IV) and its spiritual dimension (as discovered by Grof) as graphically as does Joseph Campbell. His description of the three BPMs of birth is almost disturbing and clearly identifies this experience as crisis:

> [T]he moment (indeed, the hours) of passive, helpless terror when the uterine contractions suddenly began, and continued, and continued, and continued; or the more active tortures of the second stage of delivery, when the cervix opened and propulsions through the birth canal commenced—continuing with an unremitting intensification of sheer fright and total agony, to a climax amounting practically to an experience of annihilation; when suddenly, release, light! the sharp pain of umbilical severance, suffocation until the bloodstream finds its new route to the lungs, and then, breath and breathing, on one's own![21]

In identifying the spiritual dimension that reveals itself in this clearly traumatic experience as a whole, Campbell quotes Grof directly:

> Subjectively, these experiences were of a transpersonal nature—they had a much broader framework than the body and lifespan of a single individual. The experiencers were identifying with many individuals or groups of individuals at the same time; in the extreme the identification involved all suffering [human]kind, past, present, and future. The phenomena observed here . . . are, in fact, of a mythological transpersonal order, not distorted to refer (as in the Freudian field) to the accidents of an individual life, but opening outward, as well as inward, to what James Joyce termed "the grave and constant in human suffering."[22]

BPM II corresponds to the onset of delivery. Leslie Feher, from the Natal Therapy Institute in New York, describes the infant's reactions as follows: "feelings of claustrophobia, physical torment, existential crisis and hopelessness may be mixed with feelings of guilt."[23]

There is a sense of "universal engulfment," as June Singer puts it. The spiritual experience is one of "no exit," or "hell." Antagonism toward the mother predominates.[24] Campbell is even more specific in the citing of religious imagery:

> [A]n identification with Christ crucified ("My God, my God, why hast thou forsaken me?"), Prometheus bound to the mountain crag, or Ixion to his whirling wheel. The mythic mode is of the Buddha's "All life is sorrowful": born in fear and pain, expiring in fear and pain, with little but fear and pain between. "Vanity of vanities, all is vanity."[25]

In BPM III, the propulsion through the birth canal, the child experiences "synergism with the mother as its movement and hers become one."[26] The spiritual experience connected with this matrix is the death-rebirth struggle. Here there is a clear fight for survival in the face of possible suffocation and the fear of being crushed. "This is followed by relief and relaxation, as the final 'separation' terminates union with the mother [BPM IV], and initiates independence,"[27] at least on the physical level. The mythic imagery that surfaces during BPM III is that of suffering, guilt, and sacrifice. Campbell reports that

> In the course of a therapeutic session a regression to this level may be carried to culmination in an utterly terrifying crisis of actual ego-death, complete annihilation of all levels, followed by a grandiose, expansive sense of release, rebirth, and redemption, with enormous feelings and experiences of decompression, expansion of space, and blinding, radiant light. . . . The subjects, feeling cleansed and purged, are moved now by an overwhelming love for all [human]kind, a new appreciation of the arts and of natural beauties, great zest for life, and a forgiving, wonderfully reconciled and expansive sense of God in his [her] heaven and all right with the world.[28]

The symbology of various world religions is used extensively to support the subject at various stages of the regressive therapy. The imagery of the final stage of birthing, however, after the agony and release has been experienced, returns him or her once again to the "mystical" level prior to delivery:

> [A] blissful, peaceful, contentless condition, with deep, positive feelings of joy, love, and accord, or even union with the Universe and/or God. Paradoxically, this ineffable state is at once contentless and all-containing, of nonbeing yet more than being, no ego and yet an extension of self that embraces the whole cosmos.[29]

Level I—Conclusion

Our reaction to the experiences described here may vary widely: We may mistrust psycholytic therapy generally and, therefore, wish to reject its findings wholesale. If we accept its approach, we may be disturbed by the temptation to reduce religious symbolism (much of which we are familiar with under the heading of *revelation)* to a mere projection of the birth trauma, and wonder what, then, is believable within a "purely" religious context. My lengthy exposition of this aspect of human development was intended for neither reaction. The purpose of this chapter, we will recall, is to explore our dynamic journey into the openness that we are and to which we are called at every moment of our life. What is proving increasingly more fascinating to me, as I observe the progress of human research into ever earlier phases of our beginning, is that this openness has stamped us right from the start, and that the religious dimension of death and rebirth (resurrection) marks our humanity primordially. We are indeed held in the Christ Event throughout our existence whether we know it or not. It identifies, if you will, our being archetypally. Through it Christians and non-Christians alike interpret reality. Jesus died and rose, then, not so much to establish something new in the human order of things, as to sanctify, to Christify, what already was—the human condition.

LEVEL II

The crisis of autonomy and our subsequent protracted struggle with independence, separation, and functionality bring to the conscious level the otherness of the other and our need to hold our own and find our identity in diversity rather than sameness. Conscious disconnection is necessary before conscious union—communion—can be authentically realized. Though after the birth experience the physical organism experiences itself as separate from the mother, on the psychological level a state of coenesthesis persists. The child's bondedness to the mother allows him or her to stay in a state of "cosmic" at-oneness for several months after birth. Because of a lack of conscious ego "as the center of a world of relations" as such, the neonate's connectedness to the world is nebulous, lacking concreteness. Boelen puts it well:

> It goes without saying that within the context of this undifferentiated, self-less and amorphous "all," there cannot be any frame of reference. Consequently, [neonates experience] no differentiation between up and down, between past, present and future, between here and there, between reality and fantasy. [They] cannot distinguish between the presence or absence of anything, between people and things, or between animate and inanimate objects. The perceptional world in early infancy is a nebulous phenomenon like a London fog with objects coming and going without any meaning or frame of reference. Some rudimentary frame of reference develops as soon as the infant's experience begins to differentiate. This frame of reference, however, does not yet take on the stability of the surrounding world until a conscious *ego* has emerged as the center of a world of relations.[30]

Ego Emergence

And it is precisely the emergence of this "conscious ego" that moves human openness into its second level of awareness. Boelen identifies this level as functional. It is marked by a gradual unfolding of the individual and a progressive encounter of the world as a "differentiated and structured unity,"[31] against which the budding ego gathers itself up and takes a stand in order to identify itself to itself. The general disposition of conscious openness on the second level is one of over-againstness and separation. Just as the physical organism needed to emerge from the womb for its own survival,[32] so the psychic organism now needs to separate from the all-encompassing global awareness and at-oneness in which it has been held up to now and acquire distance. The infant gradually experiences a shift, therefore, "from passivity to activity and freedom,"[33] characterized specifically as "freedom from."

The scope of this study does not permit a detailed discussion of the diverse steps toward a differentiated awareness of the world "out there," from which the infant is separated by the clear boundaries provided for by his of her conscious ego—his or her individualized center of relations. Suffice it to say that the gradual realization of one's identity as "a being set apart from other beings in [one's] surrounding world,"[34] climaxes in what is commonly spoken of as the "terrible two's": a crisis that, if evaluated in terms of suffering, seems in many respects more acute for the parents than for the child.

During this turning point of awareness for the child, there is a great deal of playful experimentation with oppositional behavior. The world appears to the emerging center of consciousness as truly fascinating as well as "other." In order to retain as well as work out autonomy in the face of it, one's ability to stand separate from it needs to be explored. When the child, therefore, enters upon what seems to be a tirade of *no's*, the oppositional behavior displayed ought not to be interpreted negatively, unpleasant though it is. It is really a playful experimentation with self-discovery.

> [I]t is only by actively setting himself [herself] apart from or op-posing [the] surrounding world that he [she] finds himself [herself] as an *ego*, as a separate individual. The emergence of the *ego* and the emergence of the environment are co-original, and constituted by their mutual op-position.[35]

We will remember Sartre's view of human consciousness as nihilation discussed in the previous chapter. As we observed there, it clearly illustrates the oppositional awareness that marks the birth of autonomy. What is of interest here is the fact that the objects (persons) against which the emerging ego holds itself and from which it differentiates itself are, nevertheless, crucial for its development. Nihilation is not destruction or rejection. The mother, or significant other, who is the recipient of my *no's* is essential for my self-discovery. Without someone to push away from or to pit myself over-against, I cannot find my "self." The ego, in its very attempts at separation, needs the other.

An interesting example illustrating this is the child's fear of the dark during this time. Darkness implies the disappearance of the objects around me. When they "go away" or "cease to be," there is nothing against which I can affirm my own being, whereby I can identify myself—even if, as in Sartre's view, I merely observe that I am not it. When objects disappear, therefore, I disappear. Their absence threatens my being. Boelen explains this phenomenon as follows:

> [T]he child finds himself [herself] as an *ego* only by actively setting himself [herself] apart from the objects, or by op-posing the surrounding world. The disappearance of the objects and the surrounding world creates the experience of the threat of the imminent non-being of his [her] own *ego*. This phenomenon, in the language of existential phenomenology, is called "anxiety."
>
> When the light goes out, and the surrounding world disappears, the child not only becomes helpless, but his [her] very existence is at stake. When he [she] is cut off from the world, he [she] is cut off from himself [herself].[36]

The child's fascination with identifying and naming things is another way by which separation from them and objectification of them takes place. The differentiation of objects not only from oneself but also among each other, helps in the quest for meaning and gives the ego solidity and power in an otherwise much too unstable environment.[37]

Movement into a world of objects, the organization and stratification of things, their separation and identification, control over them, and manipulation of them marks the functional level of openness to which the crisis of autonomy introduces the child. Functionality and the quest for objectivity is, of course, a long and complex agenda for human consciousness. It preoccupies us with particular intensity throughout our youth into our late teens, and moves us into ever more sophisticated levels of abstraction, speculation, and calculation, until this mode of openness yields, once again, to deeper forms of awareness and response to reality.

Though radical, as turning points in one's perception of reality are, they ought not to be understood as sudden break-off points. Previous levels of human openness are not completely collapsed, although an experience of their apparent disintegration may initially accompany the crisis and overwhelm us for some time with anxiety and a deep sense of desolation. After an adequate period of time has been given to experimentation with the new vision that reveals itself in the "turning," previous levels of awareness usually find themselves reintegrated into the personality. Human openness in its growth, then, does not correspond so much to ladder climbing, as it does to spiralling into depth in the manner of a dance, much as we described it in Chapter 1 when citing Maria Harris. It is not linear but circular, where what was comes back to us over and over again at ever deeper levels.

Magico-Animistic Awareness

The spiritual dimension of human development testifies particularly well to the continuity and intermeshing of the levels of consciousness. The animism, for example, so prevalent in early childhood, and the little one's magical behavior patterns connect him or her in many respects to the thought and emotional patterns of archaic society. They illustrate quite readily that the separation of subject and object and the complete isolation of things in their thingness that the total functionality of puberty will achieve is yet far off on the horizon of the emerging ego. What we are dealing with here is, indeed, *emergence* on the part of the ego out of cosmic unity. The ego does not "pop forth," but *moves forth*. As such, Level I's cosmic connectedness and Level II's objectivity remain intertwined for a long time. Only gradually does complete abstraction take over and for an extended period of time eclipse cosmic awareness.

Boelen, drawing on Jean Piaget, explains early animism and magic as follows:

> The animism of the early child affects his [her] entire being-in-the-world. Its immediate counterpart in this world is magic. . . . [T]he relation between the early child and his [her] world is one of diffuse participation. Now, this relationship is called "animism" to the extent that reality affects the child, and "magic" insofar as the child affects reality. Animism is the child's primitive perception of reality, whereas magic is his [her] primitive action upon reality. Jean Piaget illustrates this relationship with his example of children who believe that the sun follows them. "When the emphasis is on the spontaneity of the sun's action, it is a case of animism. When they believe it is they who make the sun move it is a question of . . . magic." Magic, therefore, is a mode of human behavior which through its diffuse participation in an all-pervasive, transcending, and mysterious power attempts to directly and concretely influence or control a thing or event in accordance with the wishes of the agent. Both animism and magic are rooted in the diffuse participation which characterizes the early child's being-in-the-world. Or, as Piaget puts it, "it is just at the time when feelings of participation arise from the differentiation of the self and the external world [the crisis of autonomy], that the self assumes magical powers and that in return, beings are endowed with consciousness and life."[38]

It seems that the earliest religious instincts of primitive humanity are, in embryonic form, detectable in the psyche of early childhood. In many respects we are, indeed, the microcosm of our race, and the wonder of it is that, in a sense, because of this, nothing is really new in us, just as nothing is really old.

Simple examples of the magico-animistic period in childhood are readily observable in the little one's everyday experiences and for many of us have become so ordinary that we rarely spend time reflecting on them, seeing them instead as simply childish. The life assumed by a child's doll or teddy bear is an almost universal case in point. The doll, of course, is not the only object experienced as alive during this time; the kitchen chair that gets in the way of the young explorer and is, therefore, "bad," the rocking horse, the carpet, all exude life energy for him or her. Fairy tales that endow rabbits and lions with character and personality not only contribute to the task of socialization, but honor, in fact, the child's animistic openness to reality as well. The dreams and fantasies of children during the magico-animistic period are often more real than real and quite readily can bring them to the point of "vision." Thus to assume that little Mary is lying because she claims to visit with her dead grandmother whenever she plays in the basement, or that Michael is showing off when he talks about his meetings with Jesus in his attic hideaway would be to misjudge the children's reality and to hold them to adult moral norms that are totally foreign to them still.

In the magico-animistic world view in which the child is held,

> He [she] believes that his [her] actions and his [her] thoughts
> can bring about events, and that mysterious powers are latent
> in all things. Soon he [she] extends this view and finds human
> attributes in all these phenomena, and begins to explain his
> [her] world in terms of interactions between these anthropo-
> morphic creatures. His [her] world becomes populated not
> only with elves, fairies, and other benign beings that fascinate
> him [her], but also with sinister creatures: goblins, dragons,
> ogres, witches, spooks, and kobolds that haunt him [her] day
> and night. . . . The world in which he [she] is actually
> involved by now is the world of fairy tale. . . . The child will
> have to use his [her] own playful and magical resources to

handle his [her] own existential anxieties. By repeatedly listening to fairy tales, by playfully pretending that he himself [she herself] is a witch, by casting a spell on the spooks, by shooting the dragons, and by ritualistic games he [she] scares these sinister creatures (his [her] own anxiety) into submission. Here are found the magic beginnings of self-control. The meaning of magic cannot be restricted to primitive science alone. The earliest discovery of being-in-the-world is magico-animistic. . . . By constituting his [her] primitive world as a fairy tale, he [she] arrives at a primitive understanding, articulation, and mastery of himself [herself] and his [her] world. The fairy tale is rudimentary ethics, rudimentary religion, rudimentary philosophy, rudimentary art, in short, rudimentary authenticity. . . .

[T]he world of the early child cannot be regarded as the mere product of his [her] imagination. For this view presupposes a sharp boundary between his [her] world of facts and his [her] world of fancy and dreams, a boundary which does not exist yet at this animistic stage of development.[39]

As children grow in the use of language, the power of words is frequently brought into their magico-animistic ways of responding to situations. Initially, words are not merely signs or symbols that stand for objects but possess much more power than that. Boelen points out: "They do not re-present things, but rather make them magically present. The name of a thing is [for the child] a part of the thing or even the thing itself. He [she] can bring about things and events simply by uttering their names." Boelen clarifies this with the example of the child calling his or her mother: "[B]y being able to use the word 'Mamma,' he [she] can give permanence and stability to his [her] awareness of mother, and can recreate her whenever he [she] needs her."[40]

It is not difficult for the observant reader to discover in the behavior described here and in its concomitant level of consciousness the rudiments of religion and cult. It seems that the type of openness we are discussing as pertaining to early childhood is not restricted to individual human development. Cultures pass through the same levels of awareness as do individuals but, of course, much more slowly. Vestiges of animism and magic, therefore, can be found not only in adults of today but also in advanced religions—in their doctrines and rituals. Superstitions of any kind speak of power that far exceeds the objects or events to which it is attributed. Whenever words or rituals assume disproportionate power and control, there may well be regression to magico-animistic openness. Words as such do not have power apart from the person who speaks them and the recipient of the message. When it was said of Jesus that power went out from him, this power emanated from his inner depth, not from his words or actions *per se*. Compulsive dependence on words or acts as such, expecting them to bring about safety, protection, luck, miracles of any kind, and even personal transformation, trace back to magico-animistic levels of awareness. Whenever a woman cannot go to sleep at night unless she has looked into every conceivable—even the least likely and possible—nook and cranny of her house for a possible intruder; whenever a man cannot leave his office in the evening unless the pencils on his desk are arranged absolutely parallel to each other, we are talking of compulsive ritualism of one kind or another. But ritualistic also and at times neurotic was the preoccupation of some of us prior to Vatican II with the exact distance a priest's lips needed to be from the host or chalice for consecration to be effective, or with the intention of the presider consciously directed to every last cup or ciborium on the altar for transubstantiation to take place. Might not the concern, even today, with the exact ingredients of Eucharistic bread, or with the alcoholic content of Eucharistic wine be an indication that we are not quite free from ritualistic compulsion? There seems here to be a lack of awareness of the whole and an inability even by adult minds to see the greater picture and the deeper dimension of reality.

Progressive Realism

The progressive development of the child on the functional level of awareness finds him or her ever more capable of differentiating and conceptualizing. A gradual disengagement of thought from behavioral involvement with the concrete world allows for increased ability in abstractive thinking. This is furthered rapidly, but not always painlessly, when pubescent physical changes cause estrangement from one's own body and from oneself. The body that was once one's home now seems out of sync—an object lacking in proportion, clumsy, scrawny, full of acne, awkward. Boelen puts it well when, reflecting on this time in the youngster's life, he observes that "Physically, his [her] body no longer 'fits' in his [her] environment. . . . Psychologically, he [she] feels stigmatized and socially unacceptable. Existentially, he [she] does not know where he [she] stands and worries about his [her] self-identity."[41]

The pubescent individual finds himself or herself withdrawing, therefore, from the familiar and safe environment of the home. (Often she or he interprets her or his parents' concern for her or his physical well-being as rejection.)

> Whereas the child's body-subject was a happy incarnation, the pubescent body is experienced as an awkward body-object standing in the way of this incarnation. . . . [B]y objectifying his lived embodiment, the adolescent reduces his [her] very being-in-the-world to a "problem," to something standing over against him [her]. He [she] thereby disengages himself [herself] from his [her] experiential and emotional involvement in his [her] world. Pubescence withdraws from the concrete incarnation on the bodily level into the abstractive and functional level which constitutes the world of puberty. Philosophically speaking, pubescence differs from late childhood in the fact that the shift from concrete objectivity to abstract objectivity which is already in progress becomes reinforced and codetermined by the existential changes of the embodiment.[42]

Fascination with the abstract opens the child to the structuredness of the surrounding world. How things work and how the social world is organized is of particular interest during this time. Taking things apart, collecting, and engaging in hobbies occupy much of the youngsters' time. Peer play, preferably away from adults and in secret, emphasizes order, rules, organization, structure. Setting up a secret club, for example; finding a hide-out, can excite youngsters of this age for days, even weeks. They draw up their club's charter, define membership, hold elections for offices no one needs (treasurer and secretary, for example), vote on passwords and initiation rites and, by the time the structure is all set up, have lost interest and move to another organizing task. Ritualism in its structuredness preoccupies this level of functionality, and a touch of the compulsive behavior mentioned earlier may surface here in both group and individual play:

> "[T]wo children, catching themselves saying the same thing at the same time, instantly fall into the ritual of locking their little fingers together, making a silent wish, and then exchanging the prescribed phrases before they break the hold with a ceremonial flourish and remain mute until a third person speaks to one of them and breaks the spell—if they speak without this release, the wish is lost." Even the child's solitary existence is filled with ritualism. On his [her] way to school, he [she] avoids stepping on the cracks in the sidewalk, lest the teacher call on him [her]. When he [she] looses a tooth, he [she] puts it under his [her] pillow and makes a silent wish. He [she] knocks on wood after mentioning his [her] good fortune. Or he [she] may feel a secret compulsion to touch every single lamppost, or to count every passing Volkswagen.[43]

Religious ritual, to which parents at this time feel obliged to expose their children, is of interest to children primarily in terms of its structure. And it is really useless, for the most part, to expect any depth of devotion beyond that. Their games frequently reflect what is significant to children during worship: I remember my own preoccupation during pubescence with being the presider while playing Mass, and with executing with precision the quick and smooth rotation on the heel of my foot that Father was capable of every time he turned from the pre–Vatican II altar to face the congregation. Ringing bells and spouting off Latin words or phrases correctly were also important to me at that time, while my two sisters critiqued me for precision (certainly not for piety).

Interest in religion disappears almost completely during puberty and during the adolescent crisis that follows it, when alienation from adult norms and values is finalized and confusion regarding one's own body climaxes. With the increase of difficulty in controlling bodily urges and longing, the youngster's dualistic world view reaches its peak. Only that which is measurable, calculable, verifiable, and subject to control is seen as of value. Logical reasoning and abstraction rule supreme. The scientific attitude rejects the unfathomable. In school, religion, poetry, literature, history, and all subjects whose immediate usefulness is not clear are considered boring and generally viewed as a waste of time. Competition, debate, and winning are prized. Legalism replaces ritualism, and the gang, impersonal and all conforming in its nonconformity, replaces all relationships hitherto enjoyed.

The tyranny of the gang (what Heidegger, noting this phenomenon as possible at any age, calls the "they") is all pervasive and makes personal depth thought and choices virtually impossible for the youngster. Boelen describes it well:

> Not only does the child in puberty obey the authority of the "they" rather than that of his [her] parents, he [she] also strives for the self-less uniformity of sameness. He [she] wants the same age, the same dress, the same size, the same code of behavior, and even the same sex. Anything and anybody deviating from the same averageness is mercilessly rejected as an intolerable exception. Anyone who is too tall or too fat, who wants to dress or to think differently, or who is simply of a different sex is automatically excluded.[44]

Rules of conduct and morality during this time follow the norms of sameness as well. They are generally functional, legalistic (an eye for an eye) and require strict conformity to the gang code. Today when this phenomenon extends far beyond puberty, and has been exploited by an adult consumerist and violent society, the "gang" may turn out to be a much more serious issue than a mere phase in the maturation of an adolescent. What we refer to as "gangs" in the cities of our country today is the result, in many instances, of human developmental patterns gone awry in a society that uses the vulnerable for its own gain and works out its own unresolved and unacknowledged negative energy (and negative phase of cultural adolescence, perhaps) through them. Ours is an age of obsessive domination and over-againstness. It preys on healthy moments of growth, blows up their vulnerable aspects by means of advertising and media attention, and then uses every means in its power to exploit the weakest of the weak who find themselves caught there. The natural, ontological aspects of group dependency during puberty are, therefore, distorted in our time.

For the purposes of our discussion here and to help us gain a deeper understanding of what is happening to the child in this growth period, we need to keep in mind that the co-being of the boy or girl experiencing puberty *is* that of a gang member. Here there is a natural rejection of adult norms as archaic and "out of it." This rejection is, of course, never an easy experience either for the child or the parent, but it *is* a healthy experience—the result of the process of individualization and abstraction that the child is going through at this time. Under normal circumstances, difficult though it may be, it can be endured and worked through. There is, however, for both sides inevitable confusion, hurt, and uncertainty.

Well-meaning parents often feel particularly upset with the often antireligious stance their teenagers take, and may fear that their children are losing the faith. It may be of consolation here to realize that this rejection, though its intensity can vary, is inevitable sooner or later. At some point in the human maturation process parental faith needs to be replaced with personal faith. The journey to personal faith, however, is a rocky one and may entail full-scale rejection, a prolonged period of serach, and even temporary indifference all together. A parent's or teacher's excessive zeal and upset over religious indifference on the part of the teenager will only intensify the over-against stance the young person has already assumed and will not benefit the growth of mature faith in the long run. In my own work with youngsters of this age, I have often found that discussions about interpersonal relationships, about temperament diversity, ethics, and social justice not only prove of interest to them, but also help keep alive in them the broader global perspective. "Bringing God in by the back door" is what I call it.

Puberty and the crisis of adolescence that follows is a period of progressive chaos and confusion. Perhaps one of the major reasons for this is the conflict experienced at this time between what Boelen calls the "body-subject" and the "body-object." The latter is understood in abstract terms bordering on the extreme; the former is experienced as generally in a state of chaos, with feelings, desires, and urges totally beyond the abstraction so prevalent during this time: "The overwhelming strength of his [her] body-subject's instinctual urges leaves his [her] objectifying *ego* defenseless. He [she] feels helpless, restless, and does not know where all this is leading him [her]."[45] In the extremity of conflict created in the youngster's own ontological dilemma, the stage is set for yet another turning point and breakthrough into deeper openness.

LEVEL III

Whenever an existential level of openness reaches its fullest potential, it simultaneously encounters its own limits and a period of general disenchantment sets in. As we have pointed out, human awareness is a process to which we surrender as it emerges in us in its own time. Levels of openness, therefore, do not expand at our bidding but unfold, rather, with the rhythm of life. As a consequence, crises in maturation can seem interminable. What adds particularly to the frustration is the psychic constraint experienced by the grower: His or her past is familiar, all too familiar—boring, in fact. It has proved to be effective for the concerns of *then*, but seems inadequate for the questions of *now*. These questions push the maturing person forward, but there seems to be nowhere to go with them; there are no tools to deal with them. One feels locked in with no sense of what the outside (if indeed there is one) looks like, and an ever-increasing awareness that the inside is no longer adequate. Crises call for new birth. They come upon us when we have outgrown our space. Their anxiety is brought on by the fact that new horizons have not dawned yet, and we experience not only the "no exit," but also the "no place to go."

During puberty the adolescent reaches the fullest capacity for abstract thought. This empowers reason, logic, calculative capacities, and brings functional openness to its climax. The dualism between the internal ego and the external world to which abstract openness to reality ultimately leads, however, opens up questions that abstraction, calculation, and reason alone are incapable of answering. Control over and understanding of the world outside does not necessarily guarantee understanding of the world within. The "who am I?" question, never absent, though long neglected in one's functional preoccupations, emerges once again with increasing persistency, and abstractions will not assuage its lonely cry for recognition:

> When he [she] approaches the question "Who am I?" with his [her] typical abstractive thinking, he [she] experiences a radical limitation, but does not know why. He [she] does not know that he [she] is confronted with "non-objectifiable" reality. He [she] only knows that there is no place for him [her] in this vast universe of functional and mathematical relationships. To know this universe is one thing, but to live in it is something altogether different. He [she] despairs over the meaning of life, and wonders if his [her] life is not ultimately "a tale told by an idiot." When this happens, he [she] has entered the next phase of his [her] development, the negative stage of adolescence. Little does he [she] realize that his [her] loss of identity signals the advent of his [her] true Self-discovery.[46]

With the growing loss of confidence in the abstract and functional world where one has found one's home for so long often comes an intense rejection of one's religion as well. As yet none of the institutions of the adult world have acquired a personal value for the adolescent. The reason for this, quite simply, is that the "personal" level of openness has not yet dawned for him or her. Since adult institutions carry significance in accordance with the youngster's level of awareness, they are generally seen within the confines of functionality. It stands to reason that when these confines are resented, so is anything viewed by their standards. The result, varying greatly in intensity, is an adolescent form of "a-theism" along with "a-morality" and the rejection of everything else associated with functional values. As these are the only ones the young person knows at this time, a whole-scale rejection of life in general is not uncommon. This can, of course, be most disconcerting and worrisome for those concerned with the young person's well-being, and needs to be responded to with compassion and understanding.

The theological and philosophical significance of this crisis lies primarily in the direct and unequivocal encounter on the part of the young person with the no-thingness of all things. The pain of this can be excruciating, since the youngster experiences in all its intensity the hollowing out that is necessary for him or her to embrace ultimately his or her own personhood in the empty, open receptivity and response-ability that it is.

The Beautiful Age

And when the revelation of inner depth and unlimited horizons within finally happens upon the "crisis-dweller," it is indeed grace! The suddenness of the awareness-shift is sometimes quite astounding. Young people with whom I have discussed this breakthrough frequently attest to the overwhelming and surprising nature with which depth breaks into the emptiness and discouragement, with which spirit penetrates and no-thingness becomes luminous. Physical appearance changes almost instantly. From what in my high-school teaching years I was often tempted to identify as "planned ugliness" and "willful unkemptness," the new awareness moves the youngster toward a desire for the exact opposite: cleaning one's bedroom, neatness in appearance (albeit by adolescent standards—clean jeans), are addressed with an unparalleled urgency. A general friendliness now replaces what for years had bordered on rude exclusion.

Boelen calls this period of openness immediately following the adolescent crisis the "beautiful age." This, of course, has nothing to do with the beauty of "pretty-ness," but touches, rather, the person in his or her inner depth. From there, a kind of radiance emanates and mysteriously incarnates through the eyes, the complexion, the movements of the body.

For the most part, the young person only knows that life seems better now. Analysis of what is really going on rarely takes place for the person involved in the movement. There follows, however, an intense period of playful experimentation with the values of the personal. Vision has now opened up to see others beyond their functional usefulness and to encounter them in the depth of their humanity. The youngster will find himself or herself attracted to long conversations and sharing sessions. On the other hand, moments of solitude are treasured as well. The beauty of nature, quiet walks in the woods or by the river, time for leisure and play become important. The previous frustration and discouragement with functionalism now turns to disdain, and a certain longing for radical living often has the young person recognize the "sham" of contemporary society with its consumerism and lack of concern with "what really matters." This is the age when personal relations become possible and deep friendships are formed. It is a time for dreaming dreams and writing poetry, for wonder and for prayer. Religion, whatever shape it might have taken, becomes personal. There is great vulnerability during this time and trust that can easily be abused.

Dreams and wonder cannot sustain a person forever, however. This is also the time, therefore, for radical action, for demonstrations and attempts at social reform. Political parties draw their workers and volunteers from this age group, but so do cults. At this age we first fall really in love; we are attracted to the Peace Corps or mission volunteer services; we consider religious vocations.

Reintegration of Levels

Eventually the "experimentation," as Boelen calls it, gives way to more authentic and long-term integration, and the taking of responsibility for the choices that clamor to be made as independence yields to interdependence. As during the early and middle twenties, the young person establishes himself or herself firmly on the personal level, he or she chooses a career and accepts a vocation, entering into some degree of permanence in terms of relationship and self-direction. Although issues of intimacy and identity are interpreted within the interpersonal sphere of awareness that has now been reached, there is, once again, a positive acceptance and valuing of the necessary functional concerns of existence. Previous levels of awareness, in other words, are integrated into late adolescence and early adulthood. One realistically establishes oneself in the world of functional as well as personal concerns; accepts positions of responsibility in one's profession, community, church, and family; works to achieve goals, both financial and familial, and generally aims, and ultimately arrives at, a sense of achievement. The objectives of what Jung calls the "first half of life" are in one's grasp; one's ego is established and has grown strong, and life generally seems good.

At this point it may be necessary to stress the obvious: Not every life is a success story; not every person's goals are achieved; not everyone easily "settles down" and adequately integrates his or her levels of openness. Nor are we speaking here of generalities, describing the average, identifying the status quo. Movement into mature openness is an ontological phenomenon. It befalls human beings by virtue of their humanity but with numerous variations on the theme and great diversity in terms of age and time. None of what I have described here, except for the earliest stages of development, has "deadlines" attached to it. Ours is a call into freedom. We are essentially movement—process into openness. We are a return to where we started from—a becoming what and who we *are* and ultimately owning it. The depth center of our journey, that toward which we move, is in the words of Edward C.

Whitmont, like a "pole star." It draws us, and in our quest is our fulfillment.

But stars also hide themselves or allow themselves momentarily to
be "outshone." Fixations at various levels of our journey into openness
can occur; we can enter into "forgetfulness"; we can attempt shortcuts
and get lost. We can also be held back and chained down by the various and sundry circumstances of our life. Life is simply not smooth.
Wonder can die in us and take years to revive itself. What we need to
remember is that the *quest defines us*, and that the *yearning centers us*
already in the end toward which we are striving. God, as I often jok-
ingly tell my students, is a "perceiver" on the Myers-Briggs Type
Indicator and can, therefore, allow for "variations on the theme." The
need for rush and closure is human—all too human.

The Second Journey

In "Intimations of Immortality," William Wordsworth summarizes
with great candor the story we have been telling so far about the "risk
of being human." He identifies for us also what is yet to come, not so
much by what he says about it, as by what he describes as leading up
to it:

> Heaven lies about us in our infancy!
> Shades of the prison-house begin to close
> Upon the growing Boy
> But he
> Beholds the light, and whence it flows,
> He sees it in his joy.

All this has already been told. There have been in our journey numerous deaths and resurrections, and "joy" has ultimately been ours in the
expansion and integration of our openness. Alas, however, our story is
not over:

> At length the Man perceives it die away,
> And fade into the light of common day.[47]

Much like the adolescent crisis, the turning point that heralds-in the second half of our life and is often referred to as the "midlife crisis," begins with a gradual but steady experience of disenchantment with life generally, and one's achievements and life-choices in particular, culminating ultimately in a genuine Kierkegaardian "sickness unto death."

It is not my intention here to add to the plethora of midlife literature already available. Ours is the age of midlife concerns. From workshops and retreats on this topic to full scale courses and consulting services, discussion dealing with this issue abounds and anyone interested can certainly find generous amounts of information and help.[48] Our focus here will be simply to identify the openness called forth by the crisis midway between our beginning and our ending; to explore its meaning, its call, and to send out some depth-probes into the mystery that unfolds itself as our future in the second journey of life.

The turning point of vision that announces what Jung calls the "Second Journey" is perhaps most aptly called "the crisis of the limits."[49] It is, in fact, characterized precisely by the experience of limits—often personally chosen limits throughout the first half of life—that now begin to appear restrictive. It is clear that when we as young adults began to integrate the various levels of openness we had passed through during our youth, choices had to be made and avenues taken to blend our existence into a meaningful, socialized whole within which we could function lovingly and constructively toward the goals and objectives we had set for ourselves in relation to those we loved and with whom we had chosen to live. We opted perhaps to study, to enter a particular career, to specialize in a certain field. We married, raised a family; entered religious life and became teachers, nurses, social workers, doctors, clerics. The choices we made directed us toward further choices. They gave structure and stability to our freedom, but in many ways they limited us as well. When one chose to marry a particular person, one simultaneously excluded others. Religious life excludes building a family. Becoming a doctor ordinarily limits one's choices to become a lawyer, plumber, or symphony orchestra conductor. Hopefully, the choices we made helped to fulfill us and bring us contentment. They, in many ways, identified us both to ourselves and others. Though initially our involvement with them was, in many respects, as Bernard Boelen would say, "playful experimentation" with what we experienced as extensions of our inner selves, at some point they began to assume their own stability—to exist independently of us and, ultimately, to burden us with responsibility. They became our duty, our profession, our vocation, our dependents. The realization of the limits that choice imposes on us—assuming and often "having to endure" the consequences of our freedom; the experience of burden, of a noose around one's neck; the desperate desire to break loose and yet, also, the sense that it is too late in one's life to do so, that other creative avenues are no longer open, that one is getting old and has wasted one's life— are, in a nutshell, the experiences of the crisis of the limits.

Added to this is the frustrating fact that we find ourselves, in spite of our best intentions, experiencing life, once again, much more functionally than we would ever have imagined. Boelen, describing this seeming regression on the part of midlifers, has this to say:

> In fact, many are so entirely absorbed in their work, and so eager to be in perfect control of things, that they emphasize their controlling will and calculative reason of the functional level at the expense of the cultivation of their personal world. As Jung writes, "We wholly overlook the essential fact that the achievements which society rewards are won at the cost of a diminution of personality. Many—far too many—aspects of life which should have been experienced lie in the lumber-room among dusty memories." Among these often-forgotten aspects of life are beauty, wonder, intimacy, tenderness, celebration, religion, and whatever belongs to the world of the true Self. John Gardner puts it succinctly where he states that "By middle life most of us are accomplished fugitives from ourselves."

> Indeed, most people are so absorbed in the building of their surrounding world at this stage, that they become alienated from their own Self and from the building of their own

personal world. Preoccupied by their own eagerness, by economic necessities, and society's demands to climb the heights of success, status, affluence, and power, they find that personal values frequently become casualties on the road. It seems that the increase of success, security, and comfort is directly proportional to the decrease of meaning, self-understanding, and personal happiness. The adult personality is at the peak of his [her] achievement, yet he [she] feels that everything has become routine. He [she] is in perfect control of things, yet he [she] finds that nothing makes any sense. He [she] is about to fulfill the goals of his [her] life, yet he [she] begins to ask himself [herself] questions such as, "Is this all?" or "What is life all about?"[50]

The very perfection to which our maturation process has propelled us brings with it its own demise. From within our very personality itself we seem to be moved by what I have come to call "eschatological urgency" toward something more, something deeper, something greater, less split, more whole; something more authentic that, precisely because of the dwindling time our advancing years seem to impose upon us, we are pressed toward even though we are not sure we know exactly what it really is. What we saw when we reflected on the thoughts of Dorothee Soelle in Chapter 1 becomes most relevant here: "Our need for more . . . our sense of failure . . . our awareness of life destroyed," our need for a "clean heart," even though it all seems so negative and is so very painful, is really the only viable starting point—not only for any authentic theological activity, but also (much more important and even more radically put) for mature and personal faith as such—for the depth experience of the second journey.

In Chapter 1, we identified the "pain" that Soelle sees as the prerequisite for meaningful religious activity as the pain of "our own freeing process." "It is the pain of breaking open," we said, "through the crusts of human conditioning, socialization, and stratification, through numerous cultural barriers of resistance and personal masks." The crumbling of the masks (*personas*, as Jung calls them) is certainly one of the major events set for us at the beginning of the second journey. During the first half of our lives, we spent a great deal of energy adapting our personality to the society into which we were born. The process of socialization was a long and arduous one, but through it we assumed a sense of "I-ness," of identity, that separated us from the society around us even as it helped us find a place in its structure. M. Esther Harding describes this place as follows:

> When the delicate, gelatinous stuff of the immature psyche is met by the reality of the outer external world a hardening process takes place, which we speak of as adaptation; and around the natural psyche there forms a kind of skin, a mask, by means of which the sensitive individual can adjust itself to the requirements of the environment. The initial sense of "I-ness" is largely concerned with the persona "I." In its initial stages, in the child, it is quite precarious, and indeed it may even remain so into adult life. When something happens by which the individual "loses face" he [she] feels himself [herself] to be depreciated, depotentiated, diminished. When we lose face we become little.[51]

Building up our ego as the focal point of our identity, avoiding depreciation and belittlement, becoming strong in our "I-ness" is what growing up is all about. It is also what the myth of some day "having it all together" is all about. And this is the myth that sooner or later faces us as an illusion and, in one way or another, becomes the reason for the midlife crisis. We cited Rahner in Chapter 1 inviting us to the "endurance" of ourselves as a necessary prerequisite for the depth experience of God. The midlife crisis and the journey that follows from it faces us precisely with this mandate. What has hitherto been of importance and significance to us in the building up of our world, quite simply ceases to be so:

> Life, which promised so much in earlier years, has been profoundly disappointing; one is disillusioned. And this is cer-

tainly not [or need not be] because of a lack of success in life. For it is precisely when one has achieved success, status, affluence, and power that one asks, "Is this all?" It is precisely at the peak of achievement, that one discovers that all values are open to question, and that one asks, "What is the use?" It is precisely when one has acquired everything, that one feels unfulfilled, incomplete, and depressed. . . . [T]o Jung the goals of the first half of life are the goals of nature, such as entrenchment in the outer world, professional achievement, procreation, the care of children, acquisition of wealth and social status. The goal of the second half of life is culture, by which he means personal fulfillment, spiritual life, or cosmic participation. It seems that in the process of achieving success, one has lost precisely those values that make success worth achieving.[52]

But it takes us some time to recognize our forgetfulness and to accept a rearrangement of priorities; to acquire the freedom to embrace a cosmic at-oneness with all of reality, to empty out and experience nothingness as luminosity rather than boredom. This, for most of us, requires suffering and suffering is the one thing we will want to avoid. Hence, years can go by in the midlife struggle for meaning, and the "Hound of Heaven" experience may repeat itself in our lives over and over again.

Finally, when life has utterly "lost its novelty, its freshness, its fascination, and the future holds no surprises any more," when "one has gone through just about everything: work, struggle for life, indifference, misunderstanding, human encounters, etc.," when one finally recognizes "that there is always much ado about nothing, and [that] important issues are often ignored," when "one knows how human beings behave, how conflicts arise, how human relations develop, how people try to play the roles they are expected to play," when "things begin to repeat themselves, and the uniformity of life becomes boring, meaningless, and disgusting," the stage is ready for the turning of the vision.[53] The ego, even in its strength, begins to appear as not enough;

as insignificant in its significance. The *persona* that has so well held our identity together and protected us from recognizing and facing the brokenness of our personality for so long, now begins to look like a sick veneer that really prevents rather than enhances depth encounters with ourselves, others, or even with God. Rahner's urgent plea quoted in Chapter 1 finally begins to make sense:

> Face loneliness, fear, imminent death! Allow such ultimate, basic human experiences to come first. Don't go talking about them, making up theories about them, but simply endure these basic experiences. Then in fact something like a primitive awareness of God can emerge. Then perhaps we cannot say much more about it; then what we "grasp" first of all about God appears to be nothing, to be the absent, the nameless.[54]

The crisis of the second journey is the crisis of the absence of God, of the dark night, of utter loneliness and fear, of the reality of our "being-unto-death" in its existential concreteness. It is the crisis of the hollowing out, of the emptying necessary for depth transcendence. The crisis calls us back to our quest, for it is precisely in the meaningless-ness, in the experience of the no-thing of everything that is, of every-thing that has been achieved, that finally the flute is readied for music; and slowly, so very painfully, we begin to realize that having achieved all the hopes and dreams of our youth, having gained, in other words, "the entire world," will ultimately remain worthless and insignificant without the transcendence that calls us into the surrender of our ego-power and the giving up of our control over particular events, goals, achievements, and even relationships into the stillness that underlies them all and holds them together in meaning.

> The word "transcendence" means literally "climbing across" or "going beyond" or "exceeding the limits." It is essentially a very dynamic idea. To the extent that transcendence belongs to human beings, they are always on the move and always crossing the boundaries which at any given time circumscribe

a human existence. . . . We could say that transcendence is the "becoming more," and when we speak of this "more," clearly we do not mean a quantitative more, but a qualitative more, a deepening, enhancing and enriching life, or, if one prefers, a fuller, truer humanizing of life. Transcendence means pushing back the horizons of humanity itself.[55]

Midlife transcendence is not outward directed but moves us to inwardness. It centers us, changes our perspective, and allows us to attend to what has previously been fragmented, gathering it together in our lives and into wholeness. Midlife transcendence grounds us. It calls for a radical re-evaluation of all our values, not just in our external world of work and relationships where *being* and *letting-be* begins to take precedence over *doing* and *fixing-up*, but also, and perhaps primarily, in our inner world where we are called progressively to embrace the polarities of our own humanity; to face the seeming opposites of darkness and light, good and evil, life and death, male and female; to gather them together and let them reveal to us the truth of our existence.

Slowly, very slowly, this transcendence leads us through pain, through prayer, through friends—companions on the journey, through dreams, through reflection, and ultimately through surrender not only to know ourselves more deeply, but also to love ourselves. It does this primarily because of the insight that comes through suffering: One learns to let-be, to hold oneself in one's poverty. One learns that poverty is blessed; that the hungry will be filled; that one is loved because one *is*, not because one *does*. One learns about the brotherhood and sisterhood of the human family; about the responsibility that truly loving another calls forth, the freedom and empowerment it entails. One learns of the commonality of sin and of redemption that was always there, waiting, and never needed to be earned or "lived up to." One heals even as one recognizes the "sting in the flesh," and in the healing one becomes whole.

The surrender that comes with the ultimate embracing of oneself allows one to let go of one's control devices: "You feel the managerial control of your life slipping, the stranglehold on your autonomous self weakening. . . . There is less need to broadcast your known securities or impose them on others as absolutes."[56] One grows in freedom and realizes that one is not the prime doer of one's deeds. There is a "significant shift in functional identity."[57] One begins to work out of the strength of one's poverty; the fullness of one's emptiness, not primarily out of professionalism or personal expertise. Toward the latter one is released. One's urgency changes. Life is less frantic. It becomes deeper and more dependent on God.

CONCLUSION

We began our reflection on the "Risk of Being Human," with the observation that at-onement is the story of our lives; that, according to T. S. Eliot, it is the condition of our humanity:

A condition of complete simplicity
(Costing not less than everything)

The aging process through which the second journey of our life takes us teaches us this cost over and over again in the stripping and the searing that hollowing out necessitates. It is not a "once in a life-time" inspiration that separates us willingly and whole-heartedly from functional values and enters us into the no-thing. It is a slow and repeated learning process of surrender into ever deeper experiences of freedom. At last, however, "The end of all our exploring" will indeed be our *end*, which, though it is approached every day, nevertheless carries within its final moment the culmination of all our life's choices, as in our last breath we totally give ourselves away. "We are meant to be gifts," says Marie Murphy, reflecting on Rahner's eschatology. "Our God has gifted us with himself [herself], and if we wish to achieve fulfillment we, too, must give ourselves away,"[58] so that we also might ultimately return to where we started and, knowing it for the first time, be absorbed into the Light.

4

Embraced by Compassion

*The quest defines us, and the yearning centers us already in
the end toward which we are striving.*

In his introduction to a profoundly moving reflection, *The Wisdom of
Accepted Tenderness,* Brennan Manning tells of his experience of this
end: an encounter with depth, tenderness, and compassion that over-
whelmed him quite unexpectedly one dark wintery night after months
of grueling ministry:

> *Wernersville, Pennsylvania. January 2, 1977*—It's dark and
> below zero outside and that pretty well describes where I'm at
> inside. It's the opening night of an eight-day retreat and I'm
> filled with a sense of uneasiness, restlessness, even dread.
> Bone-weary and lonely. I can't connect two thoughts about
> God. Tried to pray but quit because it seemed so artificial. . . .
> It is no joy being in [God's] presence. An oppressive but
> vague feeling of guilt stirs within me. Somehow or other I've
> failed [God]. Maybe pride, vanity, wanting recognition and
> human approval have blinded me; perhaps insensitivity to
> others has hardened my heart? Is my life a disappointment to
> You? Whatever, I've lost you through my own fault and I'm
> powerless to undo it.
>
> God, why can't I find you? My director just suggested
> that I pray the Spirit sequence from Pentecost and I find it
> painful even to pronounce your name! The next eight days
> seem like eternity. You know I just finished ninety-one days
> in the ministry without a day off. . . .

"Lord, I've done nothing but preached your Word, celebrate your sacraments, pray with your people. Why am I so
dark, empty and desolate inside? Why can't I hear your
voice?"

So began my eight-day retreat. The fatigue soon passed,
but the dryness continued. I put two hours in prayer each
morning, another two in the afternoon and two more at night.
I read Scriptures. Dust. Paced the floor. Boredom. I tried an
article given me by my director, "Enigma and Tenderness,"
by Father Kevin O'Shea. Zilch.

During the afternoon of the fifth day, I went to chapel at
4 P.M. to pray for two hours before supper. I forgot my Bible
and had nothing to read. Darn! Well, hang in anyway. I knelt
for a few moments in presential prayer (here I am, Lord; it's
all I got) then settled into a straight-back chair and began the
Great Stare—meditation.

I remained there motionless for thirteen hours. At 5:10
A.M. the following morning, I left the chapel with one phrase
ringing in my mind and pounding in my heart—"live in the
wisdom of accepted tenderness."[1]

We began our reflections on the need of inductive faith, of theology by immersion, with the example in Chapter 1 of Fritjof Capra's
mystical insight into the dancing God. We begin this chapter, dealing
with the divine initiative and response to our yearning, with a variation
on the theme of mystical encounter, a variation that focuses—not so
much on conscious awareness and insight into the Holy—as it stresses
personal poverty and total surrender.

Whenever one engages in an extensive exploration of the human
call to growth and maturation (such as we have attempted during the
preceding pages), it is not uncommon, in spite of all the reminders concerning the necessity of surrender, that the temptation presents itself,
even if only very subtly, to regard this whole process, as indeed *one's*
very own and personal accomplishment; one's *unique and primary*
achievement (not withstanding one's lip service to God, of course, who
always is "out there supplying the grace"). Along with this view, one

frequently succumbs also to all the "should's," the "must's," and the "ought's" that this mammoth task requires, and eventually, almost inevitably, one experiences the failure that is bound to accompany such an impossible responsibility. Manning's "vague feeling of guilt" and betrayal are familiar to many of us.

STIRRINGS

It is true, of course, that for authentic human maturation our complete involvement is required. Paradoxically however, as we have, in fact, attempted to illustrate throughout the preceding reflections, growth into wholeness is not primarily *our* doing. Quite incomprehensibly, it is an inner dynamic that compels us, an energy that motivates us from our deepest center and, even though it cannot be brought to fulfillment without us, it nevertheless is *total* gift and has, as such, very little to do with our achievements, with the burdens that our expectations of ourselves place upon us, with "should's" and "must's" and "ought's." Mysteriously and quite outside our ordinary categories of righteousness, the *end* toward which we are striving is already at the center of our being where it defines us even as it draws us beyond ourselves toward the authenticity that we truly are. Whether we know it or not, whether we even desire it or not, we are held in the mystery that, although it has, as Bacik points out, been eclipsed for the great majority of us today; nevertheless, it has not by that fact gone away. We are grounded in wholeness even as we struggle to gather our scattered selves. We are surrounded by depth even as we flounder in the seeming absence of all that is significant. "Deep within our spirit," says Bill Huebsch, "buried in our bones, kept as a secret in our hearts, stirring our bowels, is a great mystery yet, an energetic mystery that both draws us toward it and is the source of our power to proceed."[2]

Brennan Manning encountered this mystery on a cold January night in Wernersville and called it "tenderness." Believers through the ages have given it numerous names. They speak of unconditional love, of compassion, of mercy. "Secular" thought, concentrating more on the moment of encounter as such, describes it as "peak experience," depth encounter, Kierkegaard's "the moment," Heidegger's "being gazed upon." Theology quite simply calls it grace (Latin: *gratia*; Greek: *charis*, to identify the Hebrew understanding of conciliatory compassion, fidelity, and condescending love).[3] It sees it in numerous ways: being held or cradled in benevolence far beyond human comprehension, being utterly surprised, being healed, elevated, but also being confronted, challenged, called forth, enticed, wooed. We are surrounded by grace. It has been with us, so Rahner insists, from the beginning of creation,[4] and, in its self-giving, it embraces Christians as well as non-Christians with unconditional generosity.

PRESENCE

Sadly, however, few Christians understand grace that way. Because of the "credal baggage" with respect to the subject of grace that many of us still carry from our early schooling, "unconditional generosity" is not a quality we would normally or spontaneously associate with it. We "struggled" for grace in our youth. "Earning" it and keeping it was a thorny business and our success rate was something most of us would probably rather not think about. An introduction to grace with adequate stress on its all-inclusive and omni-present dimension is, therefore, complicated by an almost universal bias against and discomfort with this topic. Because of this, a more meaningful initial approach might be found through reflection on a neutral but parallel or twin term, such as Ralph Harper's "experience of *presence*." Harper discusses *presence* existentially, embracing a great variety of human situations. He wishes to root it at the core of our humanness—to curtail, as it were, all possible escape into the ever convenient distinctions between the sacred and the profane that have for so long allowed theology to remain other-worldly. As does grace, *presence* offers itself simply and often *in the simple*, inviting depth—what Rahner would call its transcendental dimension.

"What do I mean by presence?" Harper asks.

> I can say this. When I am moved by a painting or by music, by clouds passing in a clear night sky, by the soughing of pines in early spring, I feel the distance between me and art

and nature dissolve to some degree, and I feel at ease. . . . I
feel that what I know makes me more myself than I knew
before.[5]

Most of us can readily identify with Harper's examples. Rare
though they may be in the dailyness of our lives, they always have the
effect of moving us beyond ourselves and sparking a moment of energy seldom forgotten. Monika Hellwig sees them as experiences of
"[t]he most basic and universally available revelation." They offer the
opportunity, she says, for the "discovery of the all-encompassing
power and presence of the One who is greater than we are, prior to us,
transcending our ability to grasp, our bountiful host in the world of
nature, the silent but welcoming backdrop to all our experiences of
life."[6] For me, the redwoods in northern California hold memories of
such revelation; so does the Black Canyon of the Gunnison in
Colorado, the ancient cathedral of Freiburg im Breisgau, a masterpiece
of Romanesque and Gothic art in southern Germany, the second movement of Beethoven's Triple Concerto, Rodin's "The Kiss," Dali's
"Last Supper." Beauties of art and nature offer us an inner stillness, a
truth that has a grounding effect and opens us up to vulnerability, to
intimacy with ourselves and with our deepest yearning.

If we are fortunate enough during moments like this to share the
experience with someone dear, the look of recognition in the other's
eyes speaks of a knowledge that cuts to the center of our very being:
"we know that we know that we know," and knowledge such as this is
presence, and speaks to us of grace. Authentically human interrelation-
ship, what Martin Buber has identified as the "I and Thou" encounter,[7]
expands depth experience and turns solitude into communion. Harper
explains: Thinking of, or being with another for whom one really
cares, brings with it "an exchange of understanding and acceptance
that is the measure of love. This is how the saints felt about God," he
claims, and sees in his own experience "elements that [he] share[s]
with the saints and prophets, the philosophers and priests."[8]

One encounters the "Thou" very differently from a mere "It," for
the "Thou" holds *presence*. Intimacy exposes us to each other in our
entirety—in the whole of our being. As such it reveals depth, opens us
to mystery, and touches the divine.

When I think of presence, I think of what it is like for the soul
to be touched, the mystery of the whole self, body and spirit. I
think of the love that wants to "banish all contradictions, banish the duality of body and soul, banish perhaps even time."
This is the aim of tantric maithuna. If not union, it is an as-if
union. "He is always in my mind, as my own being," said
Cathy of Heathcliff [Brontë, *Wuthering Heights*]. It is an
identity of common feeling and common understanding.

From theophanies to erotic closeness, presence feels the
same, even if the personalities are not the same. Presence can
be explosive, liberating, revealing, quieting.[9]

Presence transcends the boundaries of space. It calls us from within even as it encounters us from without. We touch it at our center and
from there are moved beyond ourselves. Unsolicited as well as unex-
pected, it embraces and holds us, and yet it sets us free. It grounds us
and releases us simultaneously, reveals and withholds itself beyond our
control.

Presence has force and authority. It is the all-but union of
James Joyce, the *advaya* of Hinduism, the *coincidentia
oppositorum* of Nicholas of Cusa. It is not monism or dualism; it is a unitary experience and an experience of totality in
the midst of shattering differences. It is the only experience
that we can dream of and aspire to that might make it possible
for us to live untouched at the core by violence and separation, without losing our minds or our souls.[10]

And yet, so often we are touched by violence within and without.
We are victimized and even victimize ourselves. We are scattered and
torn apart. For many of us in contemporary society *presence* remains
unheeded, and grace unknown. In an age when mystery seems unrec-
ognized and we have, as Harper puts it, "lost the capacity for constant
wonder that anything at all exists,"[11] *presence* is frequently sentimen-
talized, if encountered at all, and often stays anonymous, subliminal, as
it were.

REMEMBRANCE

Strangely, however, and paradoxically, since in its deepest sense, it is our most fundamental experience of reality, it is nevertheless all-pervasive even in its absence. It is "intuited at all times," Harper suggests, "even if most of the time it is not even acknowledged."[12] He sees *presence* as "omnipresent" but as forgotten, because of our tendency to take our contact with truth and reality for granted and to assume that we have control over it. He urges us toward remembrance and asks that we examine our arrogance and its blindness, that we open ourselves up, once again, in gentle humility to "the initial awareness of Being, bathing consciousness in its reassuring embrace."[13] We need to let be and to accept a disposition of gratitude and surrender that acknowledges the giftedness in creation, the grace of existence.

As we discussed in Chapter 3, life's challenges and pain quite readily help us in this regard and nudge us toward surrender, undermining our false sense of power. But we can also reject this invitation, and many do, remaining hard and closed off. The mystics, both East and West, are perhaps our best teachers in the art of remembering.[14] They model an attitude of inwardness, of mindfulness—a capacity to be open-eyed and open-hearted. In our own time, as we have seen in Chapter 2,[15] spiritual writers and thinkers also call us to rootedness and to the meditative thought necessary for softening the heart. Meditative thinking moves us, so Heidegger claims, from onesidedness toward a remembrance of the mystery that pervades our existence.[16] It releases us toward things, enabling us to dwell among them without allowing ourselves to be addicted to them. It helps us to let them "enter our daily life, and at the same time leave them outside, that is, let them alone, as things which are nothing absolute but remain dependent upon something higher."[17] It awakens poverty of spirit, releasement.[18]

Heidegger sees ours as a culture of forgetfulness. We have lost depth and turned away from the encounter with "Being." We live in "ingratitude," as Eckhart would name it.[19] Our floundering in self-imposed complexities and speculations has barred our access to *presence* and the recognition of the grace that pervades them. "Releasement toward things and openness to the mystery," however, ". . . grant us the possibility of dwelling in the world in a totally different way. They promise us a new ground and foundation upon which we can stand."[20] They open us to silence, to that inner stillness that Rahner identifies as essential for the experience of God.[21] They do not save us from pain, for they prevent our premature escape into speculative categories and keep us from ignoring the necessary prior events of immersion into life that expose us to ourselves as we are, and call forth our deepest integrity. All "depth theology," we will recall, "begins in pain."[22]

Reflecting on Rahner's theology of grace, Roger Haight exemplifies well for us the all-inclusive nature of these events. He describes them as moments

> of infinite longings, of radical optimism, of unquenchable discontent, of the torment of the insufficiency of everything attainable, of the radical protest against death, the experience of being confronted with an absolute love precisely where it is lethally incomprehensible and seems to be silent and aloof, the experience of radical guilt and of a still-abiding hope, and so on.[23]

Releasement toward things and openness to the mystery allow us to see in these moments the breakthrough of the holy, to acknowledge them as "tributary to the divine force," to find in them the union of divine and human life.[24] Releasement toward things and openness to the mystery enable vision because they provide the freedom necessary to cut through our own prison walls and allow for the recognition of holiness within, the remembrance of being, the experience of *presence*, the encounter with grace.

GRACE

Grace is all-encompassing. It touches us in all areas of life and transcends quite readily neat theological categories and overeager intellectual distinctions. It dwells in the paradoxical—although our openness is essential for its recognition, it is, nevertheless, pure gift. The divine initiative that is so easily ignored in the hustle and bustle of our "striving for perfection" is the *embrace* that characterizes all coming to wholeness, and undergirds all our yearning.

Unfortunately, however, this understanding of grace and sacred *presence* seems foreign even to most adult believers today, including those who have had regular instructions in the faith. Though moments of *presence* may have been part of their experience, few, it seems, would readily identify these with experiences of grace.

The reasons for this are historically complex. For our purposes here, it is important to note that many of us were raised with an objectified, nonpersonalist view, and numerous types and categories of grace that were dispensed *from the outside* and could be received only upon right conduct or the valid activity of a properly ordained agent. For us, "being in the state of grace" meant something we had to work for, and "losing grace" loomed over us as a distinct possibility. We had to "have" grace in order to be able to relate to God who would not come to us otherwise.[25] The whole business seemed to rest on our shoulders. "Getting" grace was subject to numerous rules, and breaking these rules put us in the state of sin that, like grace, was neatly defined and categorized as well. Bill Huebsch puts it graphically:

> [W]e were never quite sure, not quite absolutely sure when we had it. But we were damn sure when we didn't! The rules about losing grace seemed much clearer than the ways of obtaining grace. . . . Earning grace and storing it up was the business of the spiritual life. It was the preoccupation of those seeking to be close to God. It was the primary focus of effort and the only way to heaven[26]

Heaven, of course, was very much "up there," and had little to do with the here and now, except in as much as it was *here* that we had to earn our way to it in fear and trembling.

Views such as these have a tendency to discourage people, and eventually boredom sets in with theological distinctions and categories that build on restrictions and negativity and, aside from inducing feelings of guilt, remain otherwise obscure. Guilt, of course, does not empower. The healthy person eventually rejects blind obligations "under pain of mortal sin," and seeks meaningful experience else-

where. The seeming disinterest in recent years with the topic of grace,
and even my own decision to introduce our reflections on it with the
experience of *presence* (in order to present a view not generally
thought of but hopefully enticing and worthy of interest), point to the
discomfort that this term still seems to evoke. Many people find themselves in the ambivalent state of knowing that they need grace, feeling
that they probably do not "have" it or, at least, enough of it—sensing a
general unworthiness, but wishing that they did not have to bother with
any of this. Huebsch, once again, speaks boldly to this topic:

> Many of us learned to ignore some of those childhood lessons
> in "religion" and to live with as much heart and goodness as
> we can muster. Many of us are tormented. Some of us are
> afraid of God. Some of us still count sins as we do our shoes.
> Some of us are in doubt. Some of us don't know what to think
> any more, and many of us have simply left the church because
> it was easier to do that than to unravel all those complicated
> sins and indulgences. Many people prefer to take the risk that
> God will be merciful in the end rather than struggle with a
> system that no longer seems to meet their needs.
>
> There is confusion in the church today about all of this.
> The confusion would be tolerable except that many people's
> lives are being lived in the shadow of an historical albatross
> over which they had no control. . . .
>
> The language we learned as children, the language our
> parents learned and dozens of generations before them, was a
> language of the twelfth century later frozen in time by anx-
> ious bishops at the Council of Trent, bishops fearful that with-
> out certainty, all the known world would unravel.[27]

It is a language that today leaves us either indifferent or turned off; the
language of an orthodoxy that has not allowed itself to stay in tune
with the living Word, and, because of this, has nothing to do with our
lives, appearing disconnected and aloof.

It comes, therefore, almost as a relief to note that Scripture does
not support this frozen language. "There grace appears as first and
foremost a communication of the personal Spirit of God who thus

becomes present to human being personally,"[28] and effects sanctification and healing. God's presence is seen as unconditional, God's love as gratuitous and prior to any actions on our part that might "deserve" or "earn" it. In Scripture, we hear that we are precious in God's sight and loved (Is 43:4). God has called us by name, and we belong to God (Is 43:1). God has formed our inmost being and knit us in our mother's womb (Ps 139:13). God is love, and love is of God (1 Jn 4:7). Although there is clearly a dialectic in the human encounter with the divine, and we have spent a number of pages in these reflections addressing the human side of this equation, we can never forget that *God has loved us first* (1 Jn 4:19), *and sustains all our strivings with an everlasting love.*

CHRIST

Among contemporary theologians, there is probably no one as articulate on this topic as Karl Rahner:

> God wishes to communicate [God's self], to pour forth the love that [God . . .] is. That is the first and the last of [God's] real plans and hence of [God's] real world too. Everything else exists so that this one thing might be: the eternal miracle of infinite Love. And so God makes a creature whom [God] can love: [God] creates man [and woman]. [God] creates [them] in such a way that [they] *can* receive this love which is God himself [herself], and that [they] can and must at the same time accept it for what it is: the ever astounding wonder, the unexpected, unexacted gift.[29]

All of creation from its beginning was and continues to be oriented toward this love affair with God, and this love is grace. It is not, as Cornelius Ernst says so well, "as though we were to itemize God's gifts and call one of them 'grace,' " which we could then, through wrongdoing, lose, or which could be withheld at whim. "[I]t is rather that 'grace' qualifies the whole of God's self-communication as a gift beyond all telling,"[30] a gift unconditionally given—love present from all eternity.

Contrary to much of our early training on this subject, grace is never taken away, and does not need to be "bought" back. We never lose God, so to speak. It is probably much more accurate to say that God lost us and in Christ Jesus came to reclaim us, to remind us of our heritage, to gather us back into the awareness of this love, and to show us how to abide therein: "As the Father [Mother] has loved me, so I have loved you, abide in my love" (Jn 15:9). Our redemption in Jesus, as the epiphany of God's love, is our retrieval into the Christ Event of creation. Jesus, if you will, is the insertion of God's self into history at a specific moment in time in order to witness to the fact that we are loved by a God who is love itself, and that this love affair is cosmic, embracing all of creation in an ever deepening dynamic of Christification.

In an interesting reflection dealing with the cosmic call to holiness and addressing "Our Place in Creation," Donald Nicholl describes the Christ Event as follows:

> In no time the universe came into being; and then there was time. Being and time are concomitant. But time has a different quality, a different intensity, according to the kind of being with which it is concomitant. Starting from point Alpha the quality of being, and therefore of time, intensifies as inert matter is transcended by life, and life by consciousness, and so forth with intensifying steepness until the climax is achieved (Omega) *through a self-conscious being who sacrifices himself for the sake of others*. No being, neither man [woman] nor God, can go any further; there is no further to go. That is the end of time. Once more, as in the beginning, it is no time, because both being and time have now been totally transcended: they are fulfilled.[31]

This is indeed what we celebrate at the Easter Vigil each year when we proclaim: "Christ yesterday and today, the beginning and the end, Alpha and Omega; all time belongs to him, and all the ages, to him be glory and power through every age and forever. Amen."

If humankind, as David Richo would have us understand it, is the embodiment of a "cosmos grown to consciousness,"[32] then Christ

Jesus stands for its ultimate fulfillment in love's conscious self-gift: "From the beginning until now the entire creation has been groaning in one great act of giving birth" (Rm 8:22). Being held in this cosmic travail of love is the grace of our heritage in Christ.

> The human community and the entire world in which the human community exists is oriented toward Christ and is sustained by him. . . . There is no creation except in view of Christ. There is no Covenant except in view of Christ. There is no human existence, therefore, except in view of Christ and of our New Covenant in Christ.[33]

Though Jesus of Nazareth came in time and entered concretely into the human story enfleshing the Christ in history, Jesus *as* the Christ, is understood much more meaningfully as trans-historical, embracing in his salvific presence all of creation from the beginning to now and for all ages to come. In Christ Jesus, therefore, is the fullness of creation, the end of evolution, the eschaton.

Ours is the task of claiming the power of this truth. We live in the fullness of time and are called to put on the Christ toward global Christification. Living into the Christ is bringing about the reign of God even as we recognize it already in our midst.

A HOLISTIC PROCESS

The process involved here is a unified, holistic one. As Richard P. McBrien puts it:

> This intrinsic orientation of the human person and of the entire human community in Christ radically excludes any dualism, or sharp separation, between nature and grace. . . .
>
> There are not in the human person two separate finalities, the one oriented toward the vision of God, and the other oriented toward human fulfillment apart from the vision of God. *Human existence is already graced existence.* There is no merely natural end of human existence. *Human existence in its natural condition is radically oriented toward God.*[34]

The journey of maturation that we discussed in detail in Chapter 3 *is* the expression of this orientation. Through it we claim our heritage. Its travail *is* the process of transformation. We do not mature psychologically and then become holy theologically. Neither process is an optional adjunct to the other. We, in our entirety, are caught up in the divinization process of the universe, and our freedom is authenticated only in our surrender to the birth pangs of creation-unfolding. All our strivings toward fulfillment and wholeness are contained therein and receive their significance from it.

In Chapter 1 we already reflected somewhat on this "Resurrection Insight" and on the necessity of assuming the freedom and responsibility that God's everlasting love opens up for us. Our discussion now aims at a deepening inquiry and moves, therefore, into the *how* and *why* of it, shifting to the *empowerment* that precedes, undergirds, accompanies, and embraces human freedom and responsibility. Our emphasis here is on the source of our fulfillment: It is *God* who freely willed and created our capacity for grace and freely ordained us from our beginning as radically open to him/her. It is *God*, as we discussed in the section on "Remembrance," who ordained grace to permeate "our most fundamental experiences of reality," and to draw us toward deeper meaning. It is *God* in whom rests our capacity to embrace the divine and to surrender not only ourselves, but also the universe toward global Christification. From the moment of our creation, therefore, our openness to the Holy was God's gift to us, willed by God to make our love response possible.

The modification of human existentiality that allows for receptivity of and response to the divine moves beyond nature and our natural human potential. It thus constitutes a "supernatural existential"[35] that, building on the natural human openness discussed in Chapter 2, nevertheless transcends this, moving us beyond finitude toward infinity, and giving us access to the totally Other. McBrien, dipping here into Rahner who authored this interpretation, explains it as follows:

> This "supernatural existential" is *a permanent modification of the human spirit which transforms it from within and orients it toward the God of grace and glory.* This "supernatural existential". . . by so modifying the human spirit, enables it freely

to accept or to reject grace. *Every human person has this radi-cal capacity* and many, perhaps most, have actualized it.[36]

The actualization may, of course, not always be conscious, for not all have explicitly acknowledged the Christ Event in their lives, and even among those who have, awareness of the movements of grace as grace is not always clear (as Rahner maintains: "the possibility of experienc-ing grace and the possibility of experiencing grace *as* grace are not the same thing").[37] Salvation, however, rests in our *dwelling within grace*, consciously or not, and in our *acting through its power*. Grace is uni-versal and available to all. In human openness, graced from the moment of God's breakthrough into time, lies the possibility of tran-scendence beyond nature and the ultimate reconciliation of all things in Christ. The divine-human love affair is the love song of the cosmos, and all authentic human engagement in the struggle for personal growth and integrity as well as for justice, equality, human rights and dignity, for peace and freedom is graced activity empowered through this relationship toward the reign of God.

LOVE REQUIRES LOVE

But why this love, why this overflowing? These questions may seem bold, but the only answer that seems to make sense here is that God's nature demands it—that somehow Love requires love and could not rest until it heard the echo of its yearning in the human heart.

Love, they tell us, is love only if expressed toward another. No one can love in isolation. Love in its very essence speaks of outreach, of otherness, of sharing. God's love cannot be different here, only infinitely more so. In its reaching out for the other it, therefore, almost of necessity "breaks out" into creation. Creation is the love act of God.[38]

Nor is divine freedom compromised through this, except in the most restricted sense of the word implying arbitrary choice. Freedom, most authentically understood, is the creative response to one's deepest self, one's innermost nature. The nature of God as love, then, requires cre-ative outreach in absolute freedom and divine integrity. The overflow-

ing of God into creation is the creative freedom of God in action, and
the creation of the human heart is infinite Love's free quest for an
other capable of returning this love.

> For Eckhart the human being is essentially the love response
> to the divine; the one who in a multitude of ways gathers
> God's infinite diversity in worship and in praise; the one in
> whom the universe is brought to word, to prayer, to meaning;
> the psalmist in whom all of creation praises God; the mirror in
> whom God is reflected back to God; the virgin mother whose
> emptiness receives God in releasement and births God back to
> God in gratitude; the spark where in the eternity of time and
> the infinity of space the love of God breaks forth, lights up,
> bursts into song.[39]

Rahner in commenting on God's design for his/her beloved may
not speak with the poetry of the mystics but manifests, nevertheless,
equal intensity. Human beings, he assures us, are so constituted that at
all times they

> should be *able* to receive this Love which is God . . . ; [they]
> must have a congeniality for it. [They] must be able to accept
> it (and hence grace, the beatific vision) as [those] who [have]
> room and scope, understanding and desire for it. Thus [they]
> must have a real "potency" for it. [They] must have it *always*.
> [They are] indeed [those] always addressed and claimed by
> this Love. For, as [they] now in fact [are, they are] created for
> it; [they are] thought and called into being so that Love might
> bestow itself. To this extent this "potency" is what is inmost
> and most authentic in [them], the centre and root of what
> [they are] absolutely. [They] must have it *always*: for even . . .
> the damned, who [have] turned away from this Love and
> made [themselves] incapable of receiving this Love, must still
> be really able to experience this Love (which being scorned
> now burns like fire) as that to which [they are] ordained in the
> ground of [their] concrete being; [they] must consequently
> always remain what [they were] created as: the burning long-

ing for God . . . in the immediacy of [God's] own threefold life. The capacity for the God of self-bestowing personal Love is the central and abiding existential of [human beings] as [they] really [are].[40]

SIN

It seems clear that seeing our capacity for grace within this relational context also transforms our understanding of sin. What might have been defined as "transgression" deserving of punishment, withdrawal of grace, and, in its persistence, even final damnation, is now understood much more meaningfully as tragedy, as failed or betrayed love. Sin is refusal to be open, to grow. It is the denial of freedom, the forsaking of one's destiny. The consequences of sin are separation from one's deepest truth, isolation, and finally absolute loneliness. This is so because the divine-human constitution as a dialectic of love never changes, and a denial of this can only lead to a forsaking of all fulfillment and tragic self-destruction.

Our reflection in Chapter 2 on freedom as our "dwelling in the integrity of our being," as "an involvement, a participation in a process, a disposition of readiness," as "transcendent openness," and, ultimately, as "surrender to the mystery,"[41] takes on deeper significance now. This being of ours, is pre-ordained, fixed if you will toward God. In our surrender to this fact lies our freedom—not so much as something we exercise, but rather as something we are: Freedom as a state of being is our coming to wholeness in Christ. Nor is its authenticity revealed to us as something outside ourselves as something we acquire. It unfolds, rather, within us, gradually as, through the eons of a lifetime, we come to touch the core within, and allow ourselves to acknowledge who, in the words of Rahner, "we already are by grace and what we experience at least incoherently in the limitlessness of our transcendence."[42] Our integrity, indeed our glory, lies in the creative self-revelation of God that embraces us at every moment of our existence even as the cosmos, expressing itself through us, groans toward ever greater Christification.

In accepting ourselves, Rahner assures us, we are "accepting Christ as the absolute perfection and guarantee of [our] own anonymous movement towards God by grace, and the acceptance of this belief is again not an act of [ours] alone but the work of God's grace which is the grace of Christ."[43] Sin is our rejection of this. It is forgetfulness, thoughtlessness, disintegration, idolatry, the denial of the mystery that sustains all, the "unwillingness to recognize the goodness in which we are held and to respond with releasement and gratitude."[44] Sin is the will to power.[45] It is refusing the Incarnation as it reveals itself in us, and, consequently, it is the inability to see the need for redemption.

Perhaps no one has spoken more eloquently to this subject than Sebastian Moore. Drawing on the Jungian categories of *ego-development and enhancement* characteristic of the first half of life, and *ego-transcendence toward the self* that marks the task of the second half of life,[46] he defines the struggle of maturation (our innermost process into self-acceptance), as well as the resistance to growth (a kind of ego-obsession), Christologically, once again emphasizing its holistic dimension:

> [T]he mystery of the Incarnation is not the imaginable descent of the God into the womb of the Virgin, but rather comes upon us as a *being of God in us*. The difficulty of the Incarnation is not in the dogmatic realm. It is the difficulty in a commanded *self-acceptance* that goes far beyond our limits of self-acceptance. It is the mystery of a God who comes upon *us* and loves *us beyond the limits of our ego-organized potential*.
>
> Christ is our way to the Father [Mother] only because he is the Father's [Mother's] way to us, the Father's [Mother's] way with us, the mysterious expiation of our sin.
>
> When we say with the Christmas Preface, "that through knowing God visibly we may be brought to the love of things invisible," we have to ask: what is made visible in Christ? What is made visible is God's touch in the innermost region of the soul where sin qualifies the old man [woman]. And this is the divinity of Christ: for only God can touch us there. [God] touches us by *inundating us in a mystery of Incarnation, Passion, Death and Resurrection*.[47]

What Moore describes here in boldest terms is the appropriation of our lives, our own unique destiny, our personal and individual moment in time and space, into the breakthrough of God in history. This is the Incarnation witnessed in Christ Jesus and irrevocably enfolding all of us in the eternal embrace of God's love. This is the Christ Event, the mystery of our salvation. Its rejection is betrayal of our inmost truth. It is alienation at the core. It is sin.

REDEMPTION

Using what might best be described as a psycho-theological approach, Moore sees our forgetfulness and rejection of the mystery of our salvation (sin) concretized and quite readily noticeable in the growth events of our life as we have reflected on them in Chapter 3. Sin, for him, is symbolized primarily in the almost insatiable strivings of the ego toward its own goals: individual enhancement, recognition, personal importance, and its concomitant rejection of the deeper dimension of the psyche, what Jung sees as the archetype of the divine, namely the self:

> Generically . . . evil consists in an infinite variety of alienation between the conscious ego of man [woman] and a total self in which he [she] has his [her] place in God's world. And so generically, salvation consists in the overcoming of this protean alienation. But even apart from the question of its Christological understanding, this generic statement is hedged, for the wise practitioner of Jungian theory, by an almost despairing caution: he [she] who comes to some sense of what is called the self comes under an almost insuperable temptation to claim this realization "for himself [herself]," to appropriate it in terms of the ego. . . . For the wise, on the contrary, the coming into the self is expressed only in silent contemplation, in humility, and in the indefinable benefits which the wise confer on the less aware.

The dynamic played out between the ego and the self during the process of maturation is paradigmatic, according to Moore, of the rela-

tionship between the human person and Christ Jesus, between the crucifier and the crucified. Very clearly, redemption and maturation are
interconnected; in fact, in a very real sense, they are one. Moore continues:

> Now this caution, this restricted but most precious application
> of the paradigm of ego and self, is most eloquently exempli-
> fied in our approach to the mystery of Jesus Christ. For to
> come into that mystery, I must give more serious weight than
> in Jungian praxis to the fact that I am in large part outside it.
> The articulation of *this* factor for the Christian, *his [her]* way
> of recognizing the ego in its whole political complex, *his
> [her]* way of not short-circuiting salvation, is to say: I recog-
> nize myself, in the total context of this mystery, as the sinner
> brought to consciousness and sorrow as the crucifier of the
> self, that is not "my best self" or "my full potential," or any
> other of my pretentious euphemisms, but is symbolized most
> truly by a sinless man crucified on a hill, for whose crucifix-
> ion I gladly accept liability within a mystery of God's all-
> encompassing love. As I accept *that* position, in meditation
> and in praxis of life, I may be held, in the spiritual logic of the
> mystery and under the sway of the Spirit, to a growing inward
> sense of *that which is crucified.* But as long as I live in this
> world, my life will move—in rhythm with all the complexi-
> ties of being a participant of the mystery of evil and its
> redemption—between the poles of crucifier and crucified. In
> short, the self-experience of the believer as crucifier and cru-
> cified is the most acute and committed form of that self-expe-
> rience between the poles of ego and self that is the fruit of a
> Jungian self-understanding.

Moore ends his exposition with a quote from Eliot:

> It is possible that sin may strain and struggle
> In its dark instinctive birth, to come to consciousness
> And *so* find expurgation.[48]

And here—in its acknowledgment and our surrender to the love that surpasses all understanding—lies our redemption. The death and the resurrection that is ego-transcendence ultimately yields to a gentle acceptance of ourselves wounded and yet healed. We face the sting in the flesh *as truly ours*, even as we accept God's sufficient grace, and in the glory of our own passion, that is now Christified, we learn compassion, are embraced by it, and live in it.

Self-acceptance *is* redemption. It is the fruit of the journey into wholeness. Eliot's "expurgation" lies in the interaction of our surrender to finitude and the divine embrace distinctly experienced as from beyond us even as it lights up within. Wholeness is brokenness owned and thereby healed. In the embrace of compassion, the crucifier within allows himself or herself to be held and forgiven by the crucified within and surrenders to vulnerability and gentleness. This is so because the embrace of compassion holds together our inner opposites and allows them to be *truly* ours even as it moves us toward deeper reconciliation and rebirth in Christ.

> [L]et yourself receive the one
> who is opening to you so deeply.
> For if we genuinely love Him,
> we wake up inside Christ's body . . .
>
> and everything that is hurt, everything
> that seemed to us dark, harsh, shameful,
> maimed, ugly, irreparably
> damaged, is in Him transformed
>
> and recognized as whole, as lovely,
> and radiant in His light
> we awaken as the Beloved
> in every part of our body.[49]
>
> (Symeon, the New Theologian 949–1022)

And we live "in the wisdom of accepted tenderness."

CONCLUSION

Our life is indeed an odyssey; a homecoming to the source, to Eliot's "where we started," to John Sanford's "Kingdom Within," where "the wolf shall be guest to the lamb," where "the baby shall play by the cobra's den, and the child lay [a] hand on the adder's lair" (Is 11:6,8). This return rarely happens abruptly, though the pain of it can be intense, and the insights startling. It is rather a gradual softening of the heart whereby we come to recognize ourselves as very deeply involved in the struggle of our own redemption that, nevertheless, is encountered ever as pure gift. It is an embrace from deep inside ourselves that lets total self-acceptance meet utter brokenness with uncompromising honesty yet complete abandon. And finally, it is our surrender to the story that reveals itself as our deepest truth—the story into which we were baptized, the story whose gathering point and healing symbol is Jesus Christ leading us with relentless love into conversion: the at-onement with our inmost being and through this, mysteriously, with the universe as well.

> To be changed I need *not only* to be chased out of hating myself *in* another [a process called "projection" that originates in self-estrangement and is the reason for most wars, for prejudice, violence, and condemnation of others], *but also* brought to seeing the self, that I hate, *as* other, as a man abandoned on a cross. I need to say "*there* is my life, my beauty, my possibility, my humanness, my full experience as a human which is a personifying of the universe, my outrageously ignored and neglected dream of goodness." And *that* welcomes me. That *means* me. That is my meaning. That is my symbol. That is my sacrament. That is my baptism. That is my bread and wine. That is my love.[50]

The revelation of Christ crucified in each of us and by each of us, the experience of love unto death and beyond death, of unconditional forgiveness, and total acceptance even as one knows oneself as betrayer—this, indeed, is conversion. It is life's quest. It is utter and absolute grace and its effect is deepest repentance—a sorrow that floods the human heart with tenderness, with the compassion that is God.

There is a softening of the heart that comes with compassion. It changes our vision of reality, our perception and our expectations not only of ourselves but also of others—of life itself. The vision of compassion cuts through all boundaries. It is not shocked and does not easily take offense. It knows its own darkness, its own need for forgiveness, and having received mercy, it can now pass it on. The vision of compassion is God's vision for, having appropriated the Gospel, it takes on the sin and through love ever transforms it:

A man crucified and reviled says gently to his brother: "Today you shall be with me in paradise" (Lk 23:43), and then he dies, for he knows that

[A]ll shall be well and
All manner of things shall be well
When the tongues of flame are in-folded
Into the crowned knot of fire
And the fire and the rose are one.

Questions for Focus, Reflection, and Discussion

1 / In Search of a Dancing God

1. Theology can no longer stand in isolation from other disciplines. For faith to have meaning in contemporary times the interrelatedness of theology with the natural and the human sciences, with philosophy and history, is necessary. What is your reaction to this observation?

2. How do you react to the view that "Science does not need mysticism and mysticism does not need science; [the human person] needs both"? Why is this so?

3. What do you think Bacik means when he claims that we are facing an "eclipse of mystery" in the Western world? What is the "heart" task of actual faith surrendered to the mystery?

4. How do you explain the distinction between the content of faith and the act of faith? Are both important? Why?

5. "Faith is the condition for authentic theology which, in turn, articulates it, but it can never be reduced to theology or its belief statements." How do you explain this observation?

6. How do you explain the contention that depth theology begins in pain—in "sickness unto death," in "our awareness of life destroyed"?

7. What is meant by the idea that the question "Do you believe in God?" be replaced in today's society by the question "What God do you believe in?"

8. How do you explain "theology by immersion"? How would it affect credal statements? Can you give examples?
9. The Christian God is trinitarian and the Christian God is love. Both of these statements mean the same thing. How so?
10. How is the "Who am I?" question ultimately the question that leads to God, that is, the most fundamental religious question? How does it open up the "why am I?" question, and what is its response?
11. What have you come to understand by the statement that "Sin is the unreality of God"?
12. Who is your God? Do you experience "polycratic fear"? If so, why do you think this is so? What shape does your fear take? Do you need a "revolution of consciousness"?

2 / Embracing the No-Thing

1. In light of the preceding chapter's discussion, how do you react to the observation that faith is "an occurrence, an event that gifts us, that overwhelms us, in fact, holds us"; that it is "something in which we dwell"; that it is "something we are"?
2. Why do you think emptiness and openness are so essential for faith?
3. How do you understand Sartre's interpretation of transcendence? Why does Sartre insist on the essential no-thingness of the human? Why is nihilation necessary for the awakening ego of the young child?
4. How does Heidegger understand no-thingness? How can it be seen as transcendence?
5. What do you understand by "immanent-transcendence"? Why is it that "[c]onsiderations concerning the nature of personhood as the place where faith becomes possible cannot restrict themselves to the realm of transcendence without doing a serious disservice to the reality of the human condition"?
6. How could a depth understanding of human spatiality and embodiment enhance our ministerial endeavors; our attitude and empathy toward those suffering loneliness, loss, fear, anxiety; our self-understanding?

7. What are the ministerial implications of human temporality, especially in the area of healing?

8. "In authentic ritual we proclaim the reality of our past as our future here and now. We are held in the event and stand out (ecsist) in openness toward it." What does this statement mean to you? How does it relate to Eucharist?

9. "Worship is more than attending church services. . . . Because of its communal nature, it speaks eloquently to the depth of existence." How has this chapter's discussion of our fundamental co-being enhanced your understanding of this statement?

10. With respect to the "facticity of our creaturehood," we are called to "surrender permeated with freedom." What does this mean?

11. "Death, and the birth that follows it right from our beginning, is the archetype, if you will, of our existence. The birth-death dynamic is our story." Comment on this statement, identifying how your reflection on this chapter's discussion concerning our fundamental finitude has influenced your view of our Christian story of death and resurrection.

12. Death frequently is seen as a totally negative event—as something that is best not talked about or even thought about. This chapter attempts to show our "being toward death" in a different light. Has it affected your disposition in this regard? If so, how?

13. How do you understand attunement and its effects on human openness? Why is total objectivity impossible for us?

14. How has this chapter presented human truth? Do you see any difficulty here?

15. How have you come to see human freedom? Has this chapter helped to expand your view; helped to complicate matters? In the light of the view of freedom discussed here, what is the foundational view of ethics?

3 / The Risk of Being Human

1. In the light of this chapter's reflections, what have T. S. Eliot's lines come to mean for you? "[T]he end of all our exploring will

be to arrive where we started and know the place for the first time."

2. How can the process of becoming ever more fully who we are be seen as a journey into freedom? Why does it cost "not less than everything"?

3. What is your reaction to the findings of Grof and Lake, as well as to fetal psychology in general? What can they teach us about human consciousness and the human condition in general; about the Christ Event as archetypal to the human condition?

4. What is "Great Knowledge," or Huxley's "Mind at Large"? Do you think our second journey will open up to this? How does the wisdom of age differ from that of infancy?

5. "The entire process of human life is essentially a process of birth." How have you come to understand this observation?

6. How have you come to see the magico-animistic level of awareness in early childhood? Can you find aspects of it in adult religious behavior and spirituality as well? Give examples.

7. How does the adolescent's fascination with structure, objectivity, and control influence his or her attitude toward religion? Is this reason for concern? Can you see vestiges of adolescent ritualism in adult religious behavior?

8. Why does interest in religion for many teenagers disappear almost completely during puberty and the negative stage of adolescence? What is meant by the observation that "at some point in the human maturation process parental faith needs to be replaced with personal faith"?

9. How have you personally experienced the integrating years of late adolescence and early adulthood? Did you experience idealism and radicalism giving way to the more practical concerns of life and human relating? Did you feel this as betrayal? Was it?

10. How do life choices limit us? Have your life choices limited you? Do you find this frustrating? What can you do about it?

11. How do you understand what is described as "eschatological urgency"? In Chapter 1, we quoted Soelle's view on pain as the necessary starting point for all authentic theology. How has read-

ing this chapter helped you understand this observation more deeply?

12. How do you envision the "homecoming" of the second journey?

13. What does working "out of the strength of one's poverty" look like?

14. What does "releasement" toward one's professionalism mean?

15. How do you understand the no-thingness of everything that is?

16. "Our God has gifted us with himself [herself], and if we wish to achieve fulfillment we, too, must give ourselves away." What does this mean?

4 / Embraced by Compassion

1. Can you relate to Brennan Manning's experience of desolation, guilt, and frustration? What is your reaction to the divine response?

2. What has been your understanding of grace? Were you alienated from this concept in your early schooling? Does unconditional generosity, being healed, surprised, elevated, fit your experience of grace?

3. Have moments of presence been part of your life? Can you celebrate them, live in their memory? How can they be seen as basic revelation?

4. How can we dwell among things without allowing ourselves to be addicted to them? Does such an attitude fit into the consumer society?

5. What is your response to the call toward cosmic Christification? How does it involve you? What does it mean?

6. What are the implications of a view that sees the Christ as trans-historical, "embracing in his salvific presence all of creation from the beginning to now and for all ages to come"? What, in light of this, is redemption?

7. "We do not mature psychologically and then become holy theologically. . . . We, in our entirety, are caught up in the divinization process of the universe. . . . All our strivings toward fulfillment

and wholeness are contained therein and receive their significance from it." What is your reaction to this holistic perspective? What are its ethical implications?

8. How does Rahner's "Supernatural Existential" clarify the divine-human relationship and deepen our understanding of grace as universal?

9. God's nature as love requires love and cannot rest until it hears the echo of its yearning in the human heart. We are "thought and called into being so that Love might bestow itself." This potency for God's love "is what is inmost and most authentic in [us], the centre and root of what [we are] absolutely." We are "the burning longing for God . . . in the immediacy of [God's] own threefold life." How do you relate to these reflections? Do they in any way deepen your appreciation of your existence and your relation to God?

10. We are "pre-ordained, fixed . . . toward God. In our surrender to this fact lies our freedom—not so much as something we exercise, but rather as something we are." What does this mean? How is this view different from the general view of freedom as the right and capacity to choose what one wills?

11. "Sin is refusing the Incarnation as it reveals itself in us and, consequently, it is the inability to see the need for redemption." Explain how this statement personalizes salvation history. Do you feel comfortable with such a view?

12. The crucifier and crucified of the Gospel, parallelled with the dynamic of ego-enhancement and the acceptance of the self, places the story of redemption squarely inside ourselves. What are the implications of such a view for your own spirituality and maturation?

Notes

Preface

1. H. A. Guerber, *Middle Ages* (London: Bracken Books, 1986), p. 299.

Chapter One

1. Fritjof Capra, *The Tao of Physics* (New York: Bantam Books, 1977), p. xv.
2. Barbara Fiand, *Releasement* (New York: Crossroad, 1987), pp. 1–7.
3. Capra, p. xvi.
4. Ibid., p. xvii.
5. Ibid., p. 5.
6. Joseph S. O'Leary, *Questioning Back* (Minneapolis: Winston Press, 1985), p. 73.
7. James J. Bacik, *Apologetics and the Eclipse of Mystery* (Notre Dame, IN: University of Notre Dame Press, 1980), p. xiii.
8. Ibid.
9. Dermot A. Lane, *The Experience of God* (New York: Paulist Press, 1981), p. 56.
10. Ibid. Lane does not deny, of course, that conceptualization and theory were present in the early Church, but holds that they were not seen as the primary object of faith but, rather, as its context.
11. Ibid., p. 57.
12. Dorothee Soelle, *The Strength of the Weak*, trans. Robert and Rita Kimber (Philadelphia: Westminster Press, 1984), p. 84.
13. Ibid.
14. Lane, p. 58 (italics added).
15. Ibid., pp. 58, 59 (italics added).
16. Bacik, p. 16.
17. Karl Rahner, *The Practice of Faith* (New York: Crossroad, 1983), p. 22 (italics added).
18. Ibid.
19. Soelle, p. 86. Rahner (p. 22) sees mysticism as rooted in the depths of faith, which "comes in the last resort, not from a pedagogic indoctrination from outside, supported by public opinion in secular society or in Church, nor from a merely rational argumentation of fundamental theology, but from the *experience of God*, of [God's] Spirit, of [God's] freedom, *bursting out of the very*

heart of human existence and *able to be really experienced there*, even though this experience cannot be wholly a matter for reflection or verbally objectified" (italics added).

20. Soelle, pp. 90, 91.
21. Ibid.
22. John Francis Kavanaugh, *Following Christ in a Consumer Society* (Maryknoll, NY: Orbis Books, 1981), p. 15.
23. Ibid.
24. John Macquarrie, *Principles of Christian Theology* (New York: Charles Scribner's Sons, 1977), p. 21.
25. Soelle, p. 91.
26. Ibid.
27. Elisabeth Schüssler Fiorenza, *In Memory of Her* (New York: Crossroad, 1984), p. 135.
28. Rahner's thought is here discussed by Kathleen R. Fischer and Thomas N. Hart, *Christian Foundations* (New York: Paulist, 1986), p. 45 (italics added).
29. Ibid., pp. 45, 46.
30. See Baillie's view discussed in ibid., p. 47.
31. Ibid., p. 46 (italics added).
32. Ibid., p. 47.
33. See Dermot Lane's reflections on the word *credo* at the beginning of this chapter.
34. Bernard J. Boelen, *Personal Maturity* (New York: Seabury, 1978), p. 147.
35. Maria Harris, *Dance of the Spirit* (New York: Bantam Books, 1989), p. xii.
36. Sebastian Moore, *The Fire and the Rose Are One* (London: Darton, Longman and Todd, 1980), pp. 12–18.
37. Rahner, p. 63 (italics added).
38. Ibid., p. 64.
39. Bacik, p. 27.
40. Thomas Merton, quoted here by Richard J. Hauser, S. J., *In His Spirit* (New York: Paulist, 1982), p. 50.
41. Bacik, p. 27.
42. For an explanation see: William A. Luijpen & Henry J. Koren, *A First Introduction To Existential Phenomenology* (Pittsburgh: Duquesne University Press, 1969), pp. 231–235.
43. Bacik, p. 28.
44. Ibid.
45. Fiand, p. 40.
46. Moore, p. 73.
47. Barbara Fiand, *Living the Vision* (New York: Crossroad, 1990), p. 30 (italics added).
48. Moore, p. 117.
49. Ibid., p. 144.

50. Dorothee Soelle, *Beyond Mere Obedience*, trans. Lawrence W. Denef (New York: Pilgrim Press, 1982), p. 44.
51. Ibid., pp. 43, 44.
52. Ibid., p. 44.
53. See the discussion offered by Beatrice Bruteau, "Neo-Feminism and the Next Revolution of Consciousness," *Anima* 3/2 (Spring 1977). Also, Genia Pauli Haddon, *Body Metaphors* (New York: Crossroad, 1988), especially chapter one.
54. Bruteau, p. 1.

Chapter Two

1. Caryll Houselander, *The Reed of God* (New York: Arena Lettres, 1978), p. 39.
2. Thomas Merton, quoted here by Richard J. Hauser, S.J., *In His Spirit* (New York: Paulist, 1982), p. 50.
3. Barbara Fiand, *Releasement* (New York: Crossroad, 1987), p. 5.
4. Ibid.
5. Sue Woodruff, *Meditations with Mechtild of Magdeburg*, (Santa Fe, NM: Bear & Company, 1982), p. 32.
6. Fiand, p. 6.
7. Ibid., p. 6.
8. Frederick Franck, *Messenger of the Heart* (New York: Crossroad, 1976), p. 51.
9. Lao Tsu, *Tao Te Ching*, trans. Gia-Fu Feng and Jane English (New York: Vintage Books, 1972), p. 16 (italics added).
10. Ibid., p. 4.
11. Ibid., p. 3.
12. Franck, p. 34.
13. Ibid., pp. 35, 36, 37.
14. William A. Luijpen, Ph.D., *Existential Phenomenology* (Pittsburgh: Duquesne University Press, 1969), p. 74.
15. John Macquarrie, *In Search of Humanity* (New York: Crossroad, 1983), p. 28.
16. Luijpen, pp. 41, 42.
17. Martin Heidegger, *Aus Der Erfahrung des Denkens*, 2nd ed. (Pfullingen: Verlag Günther Neske, 1965), p. 17; translation from *Poetry, Language, Thought*, trans. Albert Hofstadter (New York: Harper & Row, 1971; Harper Colophon Books, 1975), p. 9.
18. Martin Heidegger, *Vorträge Und Aufsätze*, 3 vols., 3rd ed. (Pfullingen: Vertrag Günther Neske, 1967), 2:9 (translation mine).
19. Medard Boss, *Existential Foundations of Medicine and Psychology*, trans. Stephen Conway and Anne Cleaves (New York: Jason Aronson, 1979), pp. 87, 88, 89 (italics added).
20. Ibid., p. 89.
21. Ibid., p. 103.

22. Ibid., p. 105.
23. Ibid., p. 106.
24. James J. Bacik, "Rahner's Anthropology: The Basis for a Dialectical Spirituality," *Being and Truth*, eds. Alistair Kee and Eugene T. Long, (London: SCM Press, 1968), p. 171.
25. Ibid., pp. 171, 172.
26. Ibid., p. 171.
27. June Singer, *Love's Energies* (Boston: Sigo Press, 1990), pp. 194, 195 (italics added).
28. Boss, p. 119.
29. John Macquarrie, *Principles of Christian Theology* (New York: Charles Scribner's Sons, 1977), pp. 78, 79.
30. Boss, p. 121.
31. Ibid., p. 119.
32. Ibid., p. 121.
33. Bacik, p. 173.
34. Rahner's thought is here reflected on by Marie Murphy, *New Images of Last Things* (New York: Paulist Press, 1988), p. 8.
35. Ibid., p. 9.
36. Martin Heidegger, *Sein Und Zeit*, 11th ed. (Tübingen: Max Niemeyer Verlag, 1967), p. 134.
37. Boss, p. 109
38. Ibid., p. 110.
39. Ibid., p. 122.
40. Ibid.
41. Ibid., pp. 122, 123.
42. Ibid., p. 123.
43. Heidegger, *Sein Und Zeit*, p. 30.
44. Heidegger, *Vorträge Und Aufsätze*, 1:24, 25.
45. Bernard J. Boelen, *Existential Thinking* (Pittsburgh: Duquesne University Press, 1968), p. 208.
46. Erich Neumann, *Depth Psychology and a New Ethic* (New York: Harper Torchbooks, 1973), p. 42
47. Ibid.
48. Ibid., p. 43.
49. Icarus and his father escaped from prison by means of wings they had constructed. But Icarus, in spite of warnings, flew too near to the sun—soared too high. The glue of his wings melted, and he fell into the sea and was destroyed.
50. Ibid., p. 42.
51. Ibid., p. 43.
52. John Macquarrie, *Principles of Christian Theology,* pp. 62, 63 (italics added).
53. James J. Bacik, *Apologetics and the Eclipse of Mystery* (Notre Dame, IN: University of Notre Dame Press, 1980), p. 29.

Chapter Three

1. Chogyam Trungpa, *Born in Tibet* (London, 1966), p. 96, cited here by Donald Nicholl, *Holiness* (New York: Seabury, 1981), p. 22.
2. I refer here, once again, to James J. Bacik, *Apologetics and the Eclipse of Mystery* (Notre Dame, IN: University of Notre Dame Press, 1980), in which he identifies a general loss of mystery, of the sense of the holy, that is engulfing contemporary society and from which it is the theologian's task to help liberate our age.
3. Bernard J. Boelen, *Personal Maturity* (New York: Seabury, 1978).
4. For an easily read account of the discoveries of Stanislav Grof, M.D., see: Stanislav Grof, M.D., with Hal Zina Bennett, Ph.D., *The Holotropic Mind, The Three Levels of Human Consciousness And How They Shape Our Lives* (San Francisco: Harper Collins Publishers, 1990), especially Parts I and II.
5. Discussion on the work of Stanislav Grof and Frank Lake is derived here primarily from June Singer, *Love's Energy* (Boston: Sigo Press, 1990), Chapter 11, "Awareness Between Conception and Birth," also Joseph Campbell, *Myths to Live By* (New York: Bantam Books, 1973), Chapter XII, "Envoy: No More Horizons. "
6. Singer, p. 203.
7. Ibid., p. 195.
8. Ibid., p. 275 (italics added).
9. Campbell, p. 272.
10. Ibid., p. 260.
11. Singer, p. 277.
12. Ibid., p. 203.
13. Ibid., pp. 203, 204.
14. Ibid., p. 206.
15. Thomas Verny, M.D., with John Kelly, *The Secret Life of the Unborn Child* (Toronto: Collins Publishers, 1981), p. 75.
16. Ibid. See in particular Chapters 3 and 4, dealing with "The Prenatal Self" and "Intrauterine Bonding."
17. Ibid., pp. 77, 78.
18. Boelen, p. 15.
19. Ibid., p. 17.
20. Leslie Feher, *The Psychology of Birth* (New York: Continuum, 1981), p. 15.
21. Campbell, p. 268.
22. Stanislav Grof, quoted in ibid., p. 169.
23. Feher, p. 15.
24. Singer, p. 195.
25. Campbell, p. 269.
26. Singer, p. 195.
27. Feher, p. 15.
28. Campbell, pp. 270, 271.
29. Ibid., p. 271.

30. Boelen, p. 21.
31. Ibid., p. 22.
32. Ashley Montagu, *Life Before Birth* (London: Longmans, Green, 1964), p. 217.
33. Boelen, p. 22.
34. Ibid., p. 28.
35. Ibid., p. 29.
36. Ibid., p. 31.
37. Ibid., pp. 31, 32.
38. Ibid., pp. 38, 39.
39. Ibid., p. 40.
40. Ibid., p. 41.
41. Ibid., p. 59.
42. Ibid., p. 61.
43. Ibid., pp. 65, 66.
44. Ibid., p. 73.
45. Ibid., p. 74.
46. Ibid., p. 75.
47. William Wordsworth, Ode: "Intimation of Immortality. "
48. My own favorite authors on this topic are Bernard J. Boelen, *Personal Maturity*, Chapters 6, 7, 8, where he explores the depth dimension of the second journey. Recently, Janice Brewi and Anne Brennan have rendered invaluable service to the midlifer with several books on the topic. I recommend especially: *Celebrate Mid-life*, Crossroad, 1988. A simple explanation concerning midlife issues is given also by L. Patrick Carroll, S.J., and Katherine Marie Dyckman, S.N.J.M., in a Paulist book entitled: *Chaos or Creation*. Gerald Collins's *The Second Journey* and Helen Thompson's *Journey Toward Wholeness* (also by Paulist) are also worth reading. An excellent little book of poetry by Theresia Quigley, entitled quite simply *Mid-life Poems*, put out by Lancelot Press in Hantsport, Nova Scotia, touches the very core of this period simply but profoundly.
49. Boelen, p. 112.
50. Ibid., pp. 114, 115.
51. M. Esther Harding, *The "I" and The "Not-I"* (Princeton, NJ: Princeton University Press/Bollingen Paperback Edition, 1973), p. 13.
52. Boelen, pp. 117, 118.
53. Ibid., p. 118.
54. See Chapter 1, "Spiralling Inward."
55. John Macquarrie, *In Search of Humanity* (New York: Crossroad, 1983), p. 26.
56. Brennan Manning, T.O.R., *The Wisdom of Accepted Tenderness* (Denville, NJ: Dimension Books, 1978), pp. 20, 21.
57. Ibid., p. 21.
58. Marie Murphy, *New Images of the Last Things* (New York: Paulist, 1988), p. 61.

Chapter Four

1. Brennan Manning, T.O.R., *The Wisdom of Accepted Tenderness* (Denville, NJ: Dimension Books, 1978), pp. 7, 8 (italics added).
2. Bill Huebsch, *A Spirituality of Wholeness, The New Look at Grace* (Mystic, CT: Twenty-Third Publications, 1988), p. 17.
3. Roger Haight, S.J., *The Experience and Language of Grace* (New York: Paulist Press, 1979), p. 6.
4. Karl Rahner, *Theological Investigations*, vol. I, reference: *A Rahner Reader,* ed., Gerald A. McCool (New York: Crossroad, 1984), pp. 186, 187.
5. Ralph Harper, *On Presence, Variations and Reflections* (Philadelphia: Trinity Press International, 1991), p. 6.
6. Monika K. Hellwig, *Understanding Catholicism* (New York: Paulist Press, 1981), p. 17.
7. Martin Buber, *I and Thou,* trans. Ronald Gregor Smith (New York: Scribner's, 1958), p. 3.
8. Harper, p. 6.
9. Ibid., pp. 6, 7.
10. Ibid., p. 7.
11. Ibid., p. 9.
12. Ibid.
13. Ibid.
14. See Chapter 2,"The Meaning of Person. "
15. Ibid.
16. Martin Heidegger, *Discourse on Thinking*, trans. John M. Anderson and E. Hans Freund (New York: Harper Torchbook, 1969), pp. 48–57.
17. Ibid., p. 54.
18. Barbara Fiand, *Releasement, Spirituality for Ministry* (New York: Crossroad, 1987), Ch. 1, 4.
19. Bernhard Welte, *Meister Eckhart, Gedanken zu seinen Gedanken* (Freiburg: Herder, 1979), pp. 133–139.
20. Heidegger, p. 55.
21. See Chapter 1, "Spiralling Inward. "
22. See Chapter 1, "The Need for Mystics. "
23. Haight, p. 128. Rahner's "Reflections on the Experience of Grace," *Theological Investigations*, vol. III, lists a great many more experiences of this kind and is well worth meditation.
24. Ibid.
25. Haight, p. 122. "Scholastic theologians agreed that through grace one entered into a new relationship with God, but they taught that this relationship was based on an entative or ontological change in the human person. In so doing they seemed to subordinate God's presence to existence; his indwelling to this created change in a person's being. "
26. Huebsch, pp. 6, 9.
27. Ibid., pp. 11, 12.
28. Haight, p. 122.

29.   Rahner, pp. 186, 187.
30.   Cornelius Ernst, *The Theology of Grace* (Notre Dame, IN:Fides Publishers, 1974), p. 29, cited here in Haight, p. 8.
31.   Donald Nicholl, *Holiness* (New York: Seabury, 1981), p. 14 (italics added).
32.   David Richo, *The Marriage of Heaven and Earth, A New Look at Christian Spirituality* (Kansas: Credence Cassettes), tape 3.
33.   Richard P. McBrien, *Catholicism,* vol. I (Minneapolis: Winston Press, 1980), p. 159.
34.   Ibid., pp. 160, 161.
35.   See Chapter 2, "Immanent Transcendence," for an explanation of human existentials as ontological modifications of our openness.
36.   McBrien, p. 160.
37.   Rahner, p. 185.
38.   Barbara Fiand, *Living the Vision, Religious Vows in an Age of Change* (New York: Crossroad, 1990), p. 24.
39.   Ibid., p. 26.
40.   Rahner, pp. 187, 188.
41.   See Chapter 2, "Transcendence and Freedom."
42.   Rahner, *Theological Investigations,* vol. VI, referenced in *A Rahner Reader,* p. 213.
43.   Ibid.
44.   Fiand, *Living the Vision,* p. 29.
45.   Fiand, *Releasement,* pp. 7, 8.
46.   For review see Chapter 3, "Second Journey."
47.   Sebastian Moore, *The Crucified Is No Stranger* (London: Darton, Longman & Todd, 1977), pp. 5, 6 (italics added).
48.   Ibid., pp. 11, 12.
49.   Stephen Mitchell, ed., *The Enlightened Heart, An Anthology of Sacred Poetry* (New York: Harper & Row, 1989), pp. 38, 39.
50.   Moore, pp. 27, 28.